Basic Concepts in the Philosophy of Gottfried Keller

UNC | COLLEGE OF ARTS AND SCIENCES
Germanic and Slavic Languages and Literatures

From 1949 to 2004, UNC Press and the UNC Department of Germanic & Slavic Languages and Literatures published the UNC Studies in the Germanic Languages and Literatures series. Monographs, anthologies, and critical editions in the series covered an array of topics including medieval and modern literature, theater, linguistics, philology, onomastics, and the history of ideas. Through the generous support of the National Endowment for the Humanities and the Andrew W. Mellon Foundation, books in the series have been reissued in new paperback and open access digital editions. For a complete list of books visit www.uncpress.org.

Basic Concepts in the Philosophy of Gottfried Keller

HERBERT W. REICHERT

UNC Studies in the Germanic Languages and Literatures
Number 1

Copyright © 1949

This work is licensed under a Creative Commons CC BY-NC-ND license. To view a copy of the license, visit http://creativecommons.org/licenses.

Suggested citation: Reichert, Herbert W. *Basic Concepts in the Philosophy of Gottfried Keller.* Chapel Hill: University of North Carolina Press, 1949. DOI: https://doi.org/10.5149/9781469658179_Reichert

Library of Congress Cataloging-in-Publication Data
Names: Reichert, Herbert W.
Title: Basic concepts in the philosophy of Gottfried Keller / by Herbert W. Reichert.
Other titles: University of North Carolina Studies in the Germanic Languages and Literatures ; no. 1.
Description: Chapel Hill : University of North Carolina Press, [1949] Series: University of North Carolina Studies in the Germanic Languages and Literatures. | Includes bibliographical references.
Identifiers: LCCN 49011614 | ISBN 978-1-4696-5816-2 (pbk: alk. paper) | ISBN 978-1-4696-5817-9 (ebook)
Subjects: Keller, Gottfried, 1819-1890.
Classification: LCC PD25 .N6 NO. 1

FOREWORD

This study is a revision and elaboration of my doctoral dissertation, "Studies in the *Weltanschauung* of Gottfried Keller," written at the University of Illinois in 1942 under the late Professor Albert W. Aron. It was at the suggestion of Professor Aron, to whom I shall ever remain indebted for his kindly guidance and wise counsel, that I undertook to revise the dissertation for publication.

It will be noted that the term *"Weltanschauung"* used in the original title has been replaced in the book title and all chapter titles of the present study by the word "philosophy." This has been done merely to obtain an easily read title, and the more appropriate term *Weltanschauung* (more appropriate because of the approach used in the study) is retained in the body of the text.

I am deeply grateful to the North Carolina Center of the Carnegie Foundation for the Advancement of Teaching, at the University of North Carolina, for the generous grant-in-aid which made actual publication possible. I wish also to thank Mrs. Marguerite Rust and Mrs. Elaine Miller for their assistance in typing the manuscript.

TABLE OF CONTENTS

INTRODUCTION 9

CHAPTER

    I. The Basic Concepts *Natur* and *Freiheit*, 1837-1849 13

    II. The Basic Concepts *Natur* and *Freiheit*, 1849-1886 51

    III. *Natur* and *Freiheit* in the Major Fields of Keller's Thought 93
        A. Ethics 93
        B. Aesthetics 106
        C. Politics 116
        D. Social Relations 120

    IV. Schiller and Keller 125

APPENDIX. A Brief Survey of the Critical Studies on Keller's Philosophy 137

BIBLIOGRAPHY 161

INTRODUCTION

This study of Gottfried Keller was undertaken because there is still little agreement among scholars regarding his *Weltanschauung*.[1] Despite the number of investigations which have probed the innermost recesses of Keller's mind from aesthetic, political, philosophical, and psychological points of view, opinions still diverge as profusely as rays of a beam broken through a prism. The only feature characteristic of the critical literature as a whole, its extreme divergence, may readily be seen by glancing at the conclusions of some Keller scholars.[2] Edward Hauch, Ernst Howald, A. von Gleichen-Russwurm, and Hans Kriesi expressed the conviction that Keller was primarily a political personality with a democratic philosophy of life; Erwin Ackerknecht, that Keller's political views were based on a philosophy of cultural nationalism; Ernst Corrodi, Hugo von Hofmannsthal, and Ricarda Huch, that Keller's political interests were secondary since he was essentially a religious person. Max Hochdorf believed at first that Keller had been an adherent of Balzac till 1855, had then become a mystic, and finally in his old age, a determinist; later, Hochdorf decided that Keller had been a determinist ever since 1849. Emil Ermatinger, Hans Dünnebier, and a number of other scholars felt that Keller had adhered to German Romanticism in his youth and become a devotee of Ludwig Feuerbach in his maturity. Jonas Fränkel expressed the opinion that Keller's main views had become fixed before he came to know Feuerbach. Käthe Heesch voiced the belief that Keller's early conception of nature differed radically from the subjective world of German Romanticism. One might continue in similar fashion with the lesser studies, but the point is clear: the challenge that is extended is not so much to uncover new facts as to resift material already dealt with, in an endeavor to uncover the true nature of Keller's basic views.

The present investigation began as a word study since an objective approach seemed called for, but it soon became apparent that by itself, word-study would produce only limited results.

---

[1] Webster, *Unabridged*: "A conception of the course of the events in, and of the purpose of the world as a whole, forming the philosophical view or apprehension of the Universe: the general idea embodied in a cosmology."

[2] A detailed analysis of the important studies of Keller's *Weltanschauung* is given in the appendix, pp. 137-160.

Not only had Keller often used words recurrently for purely stylistic reasons,[3] but he had also directly avoided the use of key-words[4] because he disliked labeling his ideas.[5] Furthermore, in his maturity he had become increasingly reluctant to reveal his views to what he considered an unappreciative public,[6] and felt the desire as an artist to express his ideas in symbolical pictures rather than in categorical terms.[7]

The search for recurrent words was accordingly broadened into a search for recurrent concepts whether the related keyword was present or not, and with interesting results. Two concepts which remained active and relatively unchanged in Keller's attitude throughout his life were found to have been the cornerstone of his *Weltanschauung*. These were *Natur*, the purposefully-ordered world, and *Freiheit*, moral freedom based on enlightenment. *Natur* reflected Keller's cosmology and implied a dynamic monism resembling Herderian pantheism, whereas *Freiheit* formed the basis of his understanding of man. Though not strictly parallel concepts, *Natur* and *Freiheit* were used on at least one occasion for the opposing philosophical ideas of determinism and moral idealism.[8]

These findings determined the specific aim of this study, namely, to demonstrate the active presence of the two concepts in Keller's thought throughout his life and to show that they remained virtually unchanged from first to last.

As the opinion prevails[9] that Keller's *Weltanschauung* is characterized by transition, the temporal sequence is particularly important, and consequently the study of the basic concepts has been undertaken in a chronological order. Furthermore, it has

---

[3] Cf. Priscilla M. Kramer, *The Cyclical Method of Composition in Gottfried Keller's Sinngedicht*, p. 236. Also p. 114 in this study.

[4] "Key-word" as used here has the same force as the term *Lieblingswort* used in German research. Cf. Julius Petersen in *Die Wissenschaft von der Dichtung* (I, 215): "Was sich leicht einstellt, sind die Lieblingswörter, in denen ein Zeitalter sein eigenstes Lebensgefühl ausgedrückt findet." Key-words are words which have a special significance for persons who use them to refer to their basic concepts.

[5] Emil Ermatinger: *Gottfried Kellers Leben, Briefe, und Tagebücher* (this much-quoted work will henceforth be referred to by naming its author), II, 355. Keller wrote in a letter: "Wer die Worte Natur, Biederkeit, Gefühl, Herz usw. immer im Munde führt ist gewöhnlich ein verzwickter Geselle."

[6] Cf. the poem of 1846 (Fränkel edition XIV, 247) and the parable of 1881, both of which are quoted in part on page 86 in this study.

[7] Keller's symbolism has long been recognized and several studies have been made of it. Cf. P. Settels: *Das Symbolische bei Gottfried Keller*, Köln diss., 1921.

[8] In the *Sinngedicht*.

[9] Cf. the discussion of the "romantic-realistic" approach, app., pp. 137-160.

been necessary to divide the initial analysis into two parts in order to deal adequately with the problem of Ludwig Feuerbach's influence. Chapter I treats the concepts in Keller's works till 1849. Chapter II analyzes them to see in what form they survived the transitional period of 1849 and then traces their presence in Keller's mature writings. Chapter III shows how the concepts colored Keller's thinking in the fields of ethics, art, politics, and social relations. Chapter IV presents facts connecting Schiller and Keller which support the main thesis. The appendix contains an analytical summary of the more important studies of Keller's *Weltanschauung*.

The edition of Keller's collected works used was the exhaustive and still uncompleted Fränkel edition, as it is most modern, complete, and authoritative. In 1936 this edition made available for the first time in printed form the *Urformen* of Keller's *Lieder eines Autodidakten* (1846), which are as significant for a correct understanding of Keller's early attitude as the *Urfaust* was for the views of the young Goethe. In 1939 a large number of additional *Urformen* of other early lyrics were published, as well as some poems which hitherto had not been published at all. Reference has also been made to the Hertz edition for works not available to the investigator in the Fränkel edition. In this study, unless otherwise specified, all references will be to works in the Fränkel edition.[10]

---

[10] Cf. p. 161 in this study. Full bibliographical data concerning all references will be found, pp. 161-164.

CHAPTER I

THE BASIC CONCEPTS *NATUR* AND *FREIHEIT*
1837-1849

Preserved manuscripts, including letters, verses, diaries, dramatic and novelistic fragments, of the young Keller date back as far as 1832. The year 1837 has been chosen to begin this period, however, as in a letter of that year there is the first tangible expression of philosophic attitude, and the first use of *Natur* and *Freiheit* in philosophic context. The year 1849 has been selected to end the period because in that year Keller finally overcame his philosophical uncertainty.

The significance of these limiting dates, as well as the part of Keller's life contained by them, can best be shown by a brief resumé of the events of the period. It will be recalled that in 1834 Keller had become involved in a school-boy prank and though innocent was expelled from school. Left to his own devices, he soon felt the urge to become a landscape painter. Summer visits to his uncle's home in Glattfelden enabled him to become intimately acquainted with the scenic beauty of the Swiss countryside and stimulated his artistic desire further, to the extent that he began to take art lessons in Zürich. In April, 1840, he went to Munich to carry on his art studies but was forced by lack of funds to return home in November, 1842. This setback did not immediately stifle his ambition to be a landscape painter, but allowed his earlier interest in writing to reassert itself; he had never given up this second love entirely since even in Munich it had offered him respite from the difficulties of plastic representation. In 1843 his interest in literary art finally surpassed his ambition to be a painter, as a result of his entry into the political struggle in Zürich. Here, in 1839, the radical party had lost control of the cantonal government, after it had alienated the peasantry and more conservative liberal elements by attempting to bring the author of *Das Leben Jesu*, David Friedrich Strauss, to the University of Zürich. Its defeat, however, had merely induced the radical party to reorganize and to take up with renewed vigor the fight against the dominant clerical and political absolutism. It was at this time of intense political rivalry that Keller joined the radical party and turned the poetic skill acquired from the description of nature moods and student days to the production of political poems that soon won wide-spread attention. He became the poet of the party and remained such until 1848 when, after the victory of the protestant liberals in the *Sonderbundskrieg,* the two-fold aim of the party was fully realized: the power of the federal government was strengthened and the danger of a reintroduction of the Jesuit Order was checked. In October, 1848, partly as a result of his political activities, Keller was sent at state expense to study at the University of Heidelberg, where contact with Ludwig Feuerbach, author of *Das Wesen des Christentums* brought about a crystallization of his views.

The sources for the discussion in this chapter are Keller's letters, diaries, a few incidental essays, and his poetry, all of them media for his basic opinions. The lyric poetry is the most profuse source, as 1843-1849 was Keller's chief period of lyric production.

A. *Natur*

The co-appearance of *Natur* and *Freiheit* in 1837 took place in a letter written by Keller to his friend Johann Müller. Most significant are the following passages, the first of which throws light on *Natur,* the second on the relationship of *Natur* and *Freiheit*:

> ... denn die Einsamkeit, verbunden mit dem ruhigen Anschauen der Natur, mit einem klaren, heitern Bewusztsein seines Glaubens über Schöpfung und Schöpfer, und verbunden mit einigen Widerwärtigkeiten von auszen, ist, ich behaupt' es, die einzige wahre Schule für einen Geist von edlen Anlagen ... Ich fordre keinen scharfen umfassenden Geist, keine berechnende, weitausschauende, entschlossene Kraft von einer groszen Seele ... Ich fordre von ihm das Talent sich in jedem Bach, an der kleinsten Quelle wie am gestirnten Himmel unterhalten zu können, nicht gerade um des Baches, der Quelle und des Himmels, sondern um des Gefühls der Unendlichkeit und der Grösze willen, das sich daran knüpft. (*Ermatinger* II, 4).

> Ich mache einen groszen Unterschied zwischen dem, der die Natur nur um ihrer Formen, und dem der sie um ihrer innern Harmonie willen anbetet ... Der Mensch, der der Natur und sich selbst angehört, bewahre in seiner Brust ein göttliches Gefühl von natürlichem Rechte, und auf der hellen hohen Stirn throne das hehre Bewusztsein der Freiheit! ... Ich meine nicht die Freiheit des Pöbels, noch die politische, sondern jene Freiheit, die Gott selbst

eigen ist und die den, der sie erkennt, keine schlechte Tat begehen
läszt; aber die Erkenntnis dieser Freiheit wird nur erworben durch
ein reines denkendes Herz, das seine Bestimmung aufsucht in der
Welten harmonischer Wechselbewegung. (*Ermatinger* II, pp. 5-6).

Before a discussion of these passages is undertaken, a word should be said as to the degree of sincerity with which Keller wrote the letter to Müller.

The letter belonged to a correspondence which was begun in 1835, when Keller was sixteen. It is an established fact that Müller's letters to Keller were in large part mere plagiarisms.[1] Those of Keller, on the other hand, while not entirely free from literary influences, were essentially the product of his own inner conviction. The last line of the letter under discussion reflects Keller's desire to express personal convictions:

> Verzeih, dasz ich Dir ein wenig mein Herz geleert habe, ich paszte schon lange auf eine Gelegenheit.

The reference to his share of the entire correspondence, made by Keller in *Der Grüne Heinrich,* revealed that he had expressed his own philosophical convictions, despite the fact that his style had been unnecessarily lofty and had reflected literary influences:

> Nicht ohne Selbstgefälligkeit und Absicht suchte ich meine Episteln so schön und schwungreich als immer möglich zu schreiben und es kostete mich viel Uebung und Nachdenken, meine unerfahrene Philosophie einigermaszen in Form und Zusammenhang zu bringen ... Leichter wurde es mir, den ernsten Teil der Briefe in ein Gewand ausschweifender Phantasie zu hüllen und mit dem bei meinem Jean Paul gelernten Humor zu verbrämen.[2]

Frieda Jaeggi has nicely shown the proper relationship in the young Keller of literary influence and sincerity:

> Er lauscht einer verwichenen Literaturperiode und nicht genug, dasz er die Bücher verschlingt, er erlebt sie, fühlt und leidet mit und macht seiner Begeisterung dadurch Luft, dasz er im gleichen "Stiefel" arbeitet.[3]

---

[1] "Die Episode beruht auf Wirklichkeit und die Schwindelbriefe sind noch vorhanden." *Ermatinger* I, p. 53.
[2] XVII, 141. *Der Grüne Heinrich* II. When not otherwise specified, reference will be made to the original version of 1855.
[3] Frieda Jaeggi, *GK und Jean Paul,* p. 2.

Eminent Keller scholars generally have not hesitated to accept at face value statements from the letter of 1837.[4] It may thus be concluded that the letter, including the passages quoted above, reflected Keller's own views. Now let us turn to *Natur* as used in that letter.

In the first passage, *Natur* is the world of tangible reality. It includes not merely the material reality of the earth, but that of the entire universe; to nature belong not only streams and fountains, but also the sky with its stars. However, nature's tangible forms are significant only for the feelings of greatness and eternity they can awaken in a man clear in his own mind about God and creation.

In the second passage, nature is also tangible reality, but it is again clear that outer reality is of secondary importance:

> ... ich mache einen groszen Unterschied zwischen dem, der die Natur nur um ihrer Formen, und dem der sie um ihrer innern Harmonie willen anbetet ...

Nature's real importance lay in her inner harmony which referred primarily to the cause and effect relationship, to the complex of natural laws ("in der Welten harmonischer Wechselbewegung") supposedly existing in nature. These natural laws were good and purposeful since a person who revered nature's inner harmony was filled with a feeling of natural justice and divine freedom which allowed him henceforth to do no wrong.

The two passages supplement each other. Together they reveal that the quiet contemplation of nature awakened in man feelings of the eternal and the divine. Contemplation of nature entailed not a veneration of her forms, however, but worship of the harmonious order of those forms, of the idea in nature, of natural law. Only contemplation of the great natural order could bring forth feelings of eternity, of grandeur, of justice and of freedom. The basic reality of nature was to be found in her order, in the complex of natural laws which revealed the ordering hand of God.

---

[4] Ermatinger (I, 54) held the opinion: "Der Bildungstrieb des jugendlichen Autodidakten, dazu die redliche Wahrheit seines Wesens veranlassten Keller, mit ernsthaftem Eifer auf das Geflunker des Freundes einzugehen." Hans Dünnebier, (*Gottfried Keller und Ludwig Feuerbach*, 1913, pp. 3 and 30) used the passages given above to show Keller's attitude of the time. Ackerknecht in his biography *Gottfried Keller* (1937) quoted the entire passage from the letter of 1837 under the heading, "Erste Weltanschauliche Bekenntnisse."

The same conception of nature was revealed in an essay written by Keller in the same year, entitled by Jacob Baechthold *Eine Nacht auf dem Uto*. Again nature is tangible reality:

> ... trunken schweifte das Auge über die weiten Auen und Hügel, über Wälder und Felder, Strom und See; welche heroische reine Natur, von keinem Machwerk gestört![5]

Again the importance of nature was in her inner harmony:

> Unverwandt starrte ich empor, entsetzt über diese Unendlichkeit, über diese Grösze und diese ewige Harmonie der Systeme und fand, dasz die Sternkunde die erhabenste der menschlichen Wissenschaften sei.[6]

Again the inner harmony revealed the ordering hand of God:

> Sie (die Freigeister) glaubten die Geheimnisse der Natur ergründet zu haben und schrieben den Gang des Weltenlaufs, des Lebens allein den verschiedenen Kräften zu, die in derselben wirken. Die Thoren! sie zergliederten in ihren Mäuseköpfen das grosze Uhrwerk und leiteten die Verrichtungen der Natur vom ewigen Gange der Räder und Getriebe her, ohne zu bedenken, dasz eine Hand nötig war, um das Ganze in Bewegung zu setzen.[7]

This essay also reflected a considered opinion, as the philosophical passage given above is logical and not purely emotional. The logical nature of the essay induced Ermatinger to term it "eine kühle Naturallegorie."[8]

The general applicability of this attitude toward nature for the young Keller of 1837 is shown by a passage from *Der Grüne Heinrich*, in which Keller endowed young Heinrich with an identical attitude:

> Schon früh hatte er ohne theoretische Einpflanzung, unbewuszt, die glückliche Gabe, das wahre Schöne von dem blosz Malerischen, was vielen ihr Leben lang in Sinne steckt, trennen zu können. Diese Gabe bestand in einem treuen Gedächtnis für Leben und Bedeutung der Dinge, in der Freude über ihre Gesundheit und volle Entwicklung, in einer Freude, welche den äuszern Formen-

---

[5] *Gottfried Kellers Leben, Seine Briefe und Tagebücher*, edited by Jakob Baechthold, I, 423.
[6] *Ibid.*, p. 425.
[7] *Ibid.*, p. 424.
[8] *Ermatinger* I, 103.

reichtum vergessen kann, der oft eigentlich mehr ein Barockes als Schönes ist.⁹

In this passage, nature is also possessed of "äuszern Formenreichtum," but her importance is "das wahre Schöne," "(das) Leben und Bedeutung der Dinge," "Gesundheit und volle Entwicklung,"—in a word, the inner harmony or divinely ordered state of nature.

Natur then, in Keller's *Weltanschauung* of 1837, was the universe of tangible forms. But her basic reality lay not in her form, but in her order which reflected the reality of God. Nature's importance—and one may say her philosophical reality—lay in her divine idea, in the harmonious order of her forms. (It may seem to some readers at this point that in the letter of 1837, God was a more fundamental concept than *Natur*. In a sense this is undoubtedly true. But psychologically considered it must be admitted that Keller experienced God in nature and that his religious experience was a part of his nature experience. As developed above, the awareness of God is implicit in the concept *Natur*.)

After 1837 Keller expressed his nature ideas and feelings most frequently in his poetry. The few poems written by Keller prior to his departure for Munich in 1840 were for the most part nature poems. Though student themes predominated in his poetry during his Munich years, he also wrote "In eines Armen Gärtchen" which told the tragic story of a broken love in terms of a butterfly and a rose. After the return home, his production of nature lyrics became profuse and remained so till the end of 1845.

---

⁹ XVI, 44. *Der Grüne Heinrich* I. The present study accepts with one qualification the consensus of scholarly opinion that the work was a valid statement of Keller's views. *Der Grüne Heinrich* was written in the burning disappointment of unrequited love, and analysts of Keller's psychology agree that the work was a reflection of his powerful need for self-expression and inner release. Paul Foucar expressed the general attitude of scholars in the words: "Die Lebensauffassung des Dichters . . . als deren bewuszte Ausprägung das Kunstwerk gelten musz." Cf. also E. Hauch, *Gottfried Keller as a Democratic Idealist*, 57; R. Huch, *Gottfried Keller*, p. 19; E. Neis, *Romantik und Realismus in den Prosawerken Gottfried Kellers*, pp. 27-33; H. Dünnebier, *op. cit.*, pp. 123-151.

The one qualification has to do with young Heinrich's conception of freewill. It will later be seen that this conception does not coincide completely with that of the young Keller. The explanation for this disagreement lies in the fact that though the novel was largely autobiographical in nature, it was also a *Tendenzroman* which sought to show the development of a young man from a subjective outlook to an objective *Weltanschauung*. It suited the author's purposes to distort the youth's early conception of freewill into an absolute freewill such as was held by the more extreme German Romanticists. Cf. H. Dünnebier, *op cit.*, p. 68.

From then till 1849 ethical and patriotic sentiments generally accompanied nature moods in his poetry.

The number of these nature lyrics is larger than was formerly supposed. The recent publication of Keller's *Nachgelassene Gedichte* in the Fränkel edition, volumes XIII and XIV, has swelled considerably the relatively small number of lyrics found in the *Buch der Natur* of the *Gesammelte Gedichte* (1883).

Many of Keller's nature lyrics merely reflected his deep joy in nature, and only occasionally is there an explicit reference in word or picture to the teleologic element in nature to indicate that Keller's real interest was not so much in the "malerische" effect as in the appreciation of "das wahre Schöne" and in the understanding of the "Leben und Bedeutung der Dinge." An example such as the following is rare:

> Saget mir ihr Sterne Gottes
> Die ihr dort im Weltenraume
> Wunderbare Wege wandelt,
> Uranfänglich, ewiglich!
> . . .
> Und die Sonnen, die ihr jubelnd,
> Harmonienvoll umkreiset,
> Werden sie euch auch verdunkelt
> Und geschwärzt vom falschen Neid?
> (XIII, 74 "Stunden," 1843)

More frequent are examples which by implication stress "Entwicklung" and "Leben":

> Tausendfach wollen die Blumen entriegeln
> Aus ihrer Brust den gefangenen Gott.
> (XIV, 8, "Morgen," 1845)

> Am offenen Fenster blühen dunkle Nelken
> Vielleicht die letzte Nacht vor ihrem Welken . . . .
> (XIV, 21, "Nachtfalter," 1844)

> Das ist doch eine üppige Zeit,
> Wo alles so schweigend blüht und glüht . . .
> (XIV, 36, "Sommer," 1844)

> Wie nun alles stirbt und endet
> Und das letzte Rosenblatt
> Müd sich an die Erde wendet
> In die kühle Ruhestatt!
> (XIII, 64, "Herbst," 1845)

> Strahlende Unsterblichkeit
> Wandelt durch die Lüfte.
> (XIV, 30, "Unter Sternen," 1843)

> Wie strahlet ihr im Morgenschein,
> Du rosig Kind, der Blütenbaum
> Und dieser Brunnen frisch und rein—
> Ein schönres Kleeblatt gibt es kaum.

> Wie dreifach lieblich hat Natur
> In euch sich lächelnd offenbart!
> Aus deinem Aug' grüszt ihre Spur
> Des Wandrers stille Morgenfahrt.
> (I, 31, "Am Brunnen," before 1846)

> Ich sinne, wo in weiter Welt
> Jetzt sterben mag ein Menschenkind?
> Und ob vielleicht den Einzug hält
> Ganz still ein lächelnd Heldenkind?
> (XIV, 28, "Nacht," 1844)

A number of Keller's nature lyrics deal solely with his profound religious experience. Though these seldom refer to the natural order directly, they illuminate Keller's conception of nature as purposeful by showing that he believed God to be in nature. Thus, in "Frühlingsanfang" God is apparent in the birth of Spring:

> Gott schlägt den Tabernakel auf
> In allen jungen Wäldern,
> Der Weihrauch steigt zum Himmel auf
> Rings aus Gebirg und Feldern.
> (XIII, 58, 1844)

In the hush of night, especially, the poet found God in nature. In "Nacht V" he felt as if God were going to make himself known to him:

> Doch wie nun auf dem Erdental
> Ein absolutes Schweigen ruht;
> Ich fühle mich so leicht zumal
> Und wie die Welt so still und gut.

> Der letzte leise Schmerz und Spott
> Verschwindet aus des Herzens Grund;
> Mir ist, als tät der alte Gott
> Mir endlich seinen Namen kund.
> (XIV, 29, 1844)

In "Unter Sternen" the poet feels a unity with God:

> Mag die Sonne nun bislang
> Andern Zonen scheinen:
> Hier fühl ich Zusammenhang
> Mit dem All und Einen!
> (XIV, 30, 1843)

So strong was Keller's religious experience out in the open under the endless night-sky that he turned to nature, when tormented by doubt, to rediscover his God:

> O ew'ge Nacht; o blaue klare Nacht,
> Und doch so schwer und undurchdringlich dunkel!
> ... Ich werf mein blutend Herz in diesen Schlund,
> Ins Meer der Nacht, und angle nach dem Gotte!
> (XIII, 50, "Nachtlied," 1844)

The relation of Keller's religious experience in nature to his conception of nature as a harmonious order of laws is especially apparent from the poem "Abend," in which the religious doubts of the poet are appeased by the purposeful regularity in nature. At first the poet is in despair because the sun will not remain to console him, but soon the rising moon shows him the sublime purposefulness of all things and he becomes devoutly thankful:

> . . .
> Der du im Unsichtbaren schwebst,
> Doch immer in mir widerklingend!
> Der du die goldnen Brücken webst,
> Von Welten sie zu Welten schwingend,
> Du hast ein Liebesband gewoben
> Mir um das Herz so alt und krank.
> Du hast mich aus dem Staub erhoben—
> Du groszer Weber, habe Dank.
> (XIV, 15, 1844)

Keller's references to nature's order were for the most part indirect. On a few occasions, however, he wrote poems explicitly to revere that order. In 1838 a little poem, termed by Fränkel the first formulation of one of Keller's basic attitudes (XIII, 375), voiced an aversion for everything not normal and natural, i.e., not in accordance with natural law:

> Misztraue allem Auszerordentlichen,
> Denn ungesegnet lebt das Ungemeine,
> Sich selbst zur Qual und Andern zur Verwirrung.
> Das Ungemeine ist das Ungelungene,
> Das nicht vermochte grosz genug zu denken,
> So einfach still zu sein wie die Natur,
> Und sich für gröszer achtend schlechter ward!
> (XIII, 9)

In July, 1843, Keller formulated a plan for a poem which was to eulogize the harmony of nature. All the flowers—anxious to see one another in their splendor, all at the same time—decide to bloom together in a certain Fall:

> Dieser Herbst kommt, und in feenhafter Menge und Mannigfaltigkeit spriesen die Blüten des ganzen Jahres auf einmal hervor. Grosze Pracht. Aber bald entbehrt diese Blume das, jene etwas anderes, und alle, bis auf die Herbstblumen, fühlen sich mitten in dem üppigen zaubrischen Leben unglücklich. (*Ermatinger* II, 110)

The divine, ordering hand had already placed the flowers where they were best suited.

In November, 1843, the most glowing praise for the harmony in nature was expressed in "Lebenslust":

> Fischlein im Rheine,
> Röslein im Garten,
> Vögel im Haine
> Vielerlei Arten,
> Sternlein am Himmel,
> Glänzend Gewimmel
> Schwimmen und blühen,
> Singen und glühen,
> Und auf den Bergen der Quellen Schatz—
> Jegliches ist an dem besten Platz!
> (XIII, 79)

The revised form of "Lebenslust," which was included in the *Gesammelte Gedichte* as a separate poem, began as follows:

> Wie doch ein jeglich Leben
> Sein ganzes Sein erfüllt
> Und all sein durstig Streben
> Im vollen Becher stillt!
>
> Die Rosen blühen im Garten
> Wie spät der Lenz auch kommt;
> Drum magst du still erwarten
> Dein Stündlein, so dir frommt!

> In dunkler Nacht die Sterne
> Glühn erst am Himmelshaus,
> Und sei sie noch so ferne,
> Die Nacht bleibt dir nicht aus!
> (XIII, 80)

There can be little doubt, then, that *Natur* was of basic importance to Keller's conception of reality, and that, despite his profound aesthetic and religious experiences in nature, *Natur* was not arbitrarily romantic but expressive of an outlook similar to Herderian pantheism.[10] Tangible nature was evolving according to eternal, universal, purposeful laws which reflected the hand of God.

Some aspects of *Natur*, however, still require clarification. For example, though the laws of nature were clearly dynamic, what was the essence of the totality of nature? How closely did Keller before 1849 come to identify God with nature? Was man a part of the natural order, as indicated in the letter of 1837? If so, what was his destiny on earth and what became of him after death?

Taking the problem of man first, it will be noted that the revised version of "Lebenslust" reaffirmed Keller's conviction that man, too, belonged in the natural order. This conviction had remained strong within him ever since 1837. Even in the dark days in Munich, Keller had cheered both his mother and himself with the repeated assurance that his "Schicksal so gut in Gottes Hand steht, als das jedes andern Menschen,[11] that he had "keine Ursache an der Vorsehung zu zweifeln."[12] He had sought consolation several times in the belief that it was the natural lot of an artist to undergo tribulations at first. Others had had "das gleiche Schicksal" and had succeeded; he would not be an exception to the rule.[13]

Keller's belief of the 1840's that man belonged to nature's order was till recently obscured, as many poems seemed to stress

---

[10] Keller's stress on feeling as the portal to the divine is, of course, not too far removed from the nature philosophy of the early German romanticists. His emphasis on the "feeling of eternity" reminds one of the "inner unity" of Novalis and the "universality" of Schleiermacher. However, Keller was an artist, like Goethe, who for all his idealism could not consider "Die Natur . . . mit ihren tausend Bildern und Schönheiten" as merely phenomenological. Though God was spirit and underlying reality, nature's forms were not a purely subjective interpretation of reality due to the nature of the human mind. The divine was revealed *in* the tangible world, in the purposeful and harmonious relationship of its forms. Thus Keller stood closer to Herder and Goethe than to the Romanticists.

[11] *Ermatinger* II, 69. Letter of August, 1841.
[12] *Ermatinger* II, p. 71. Letter of September, 1841.
[13] *Ermatinger* II, 79. Letter of November, 1841.

the absolute freewill of man with no mention of the need to obey natural law. Thus in the poem "Trübes Wetter" of 1844 the concluding lines read:

> Ich aber, mein bewusztes Ich,
> Beschau das Spiel in stiller Ruh,
> Und meine Seele rüstet sich
> *Zum Kampfe mit dem Schicksal zu.*
> (I, 68, *Gesammelte Gedichte*) (my italics)

Such defiance of destiny is directly opposed to the attitude of the nature devotee as manifested in the preceding poems. However, Jonas Fränkel, in his edition of Keller's *Nachgelassene Gedichte* (1936-1939), revealed that August Adolf Ludwig Follen had occasioned the change.[14] Fränkel showed that Follen had not hesitated to alter poems of two other writers, one of whom was August Wilhelm Schlegel, and that Follen adhered to a subjective idealism which would explain lines such as the above. Follen was Keller's patron and publisher, and the youthful poet had had no choice. He submitted, though not without inner bitterness, to alteration of his verse.[15] The *Nachgelassene Gedichte* contain the original version of the verse quoted above:

> Ich aber schaue innerlich
> Still lächelnd zu in guter Ruh,
> Und meine Seele rüstet sich
> *Ergebend ihrem Schicksal zu.*
> (my italics)[16]

---

[14] XIV, xv-xxxii, especially xxiv.

[15] It is important to note that both of the living Keller biographers, Ermatinger and Ackerknecht, felt that Follen had done Keller a great service in editing his poetry, as they both were of the opinion that Keller was a romanticist in attitude till 1849. Neither scholar apparently realized that *he was accepting Follen's Weltanschauung in place of Keller's*. Thus Ackerknecht (*Gottfried Keller*, p. 109) had said: "Keller musz das Vertrauen dankbar empfunden haben, das ihm Follen durch seine Mitwirkung an der Ausfeilung erwies. Da zahlreiche Niederschriften mit dessen eigenhändigen Aenderungen und Einwendungen sowie Aufzeichnungen Kellers darüber erhalten sind, können wir uns heute noch davon überzeugen, wie gründlich er die Verse das jungen Dichters in bezug auf ihre technische Sauberkeit, aber auch auf ihre Bilderkraft durchgearbeitet habe. In einem Brief an Keller vom Frühjahr 1846 vergleicht er sich geradezu, auf Jean Pauls 'Titan' anspielend, mit einem Münzstock." Ermatinger (I, 135) noted that "Keller hat sich später sehr kühl über Follens und der anderen Freunde kritischen Rat geäuszert und ihnen vorgeworfen, dasz sie einen zu wenig feinen Masztab an sein Schaffen angelegt; lediglich die tendenziöspolitische Seite seiner Produktion habe ihm schnell Freund und Gönner verschafft." But Ermatinger remained convinced that "Follens Urteil und Hilfe (war) eine unschätzbare Förderung."

[16] XIV, 57. Fränkel recognized the significant difference between the two versions of this stanza: "Die ganze Schluszstrophe, die des Dichters Haltung ins Gegenteil kehrt, trägt deutlich Follensche Gepräge." (XIV, 322)

Here is the attitude toward nature which Keller had repeatedly expressed, an attitude justifying the use of the phrase, "still lächelnd ... in guter Ruh," which would have been nonsensical in the previous version. A similar alteration, even more obvious to a person acquainted with Keller, which distorted meaning and stressed an absolute freewill was made in the poem "Erkenntnis." The altered lines read:

> Tu frei und offen was du nicht willst lassen
> Doch wandle streng auf selbstbeschränkten Wegen.
> (I, 145, *Gesammelte Gedichte*, 184-)

The "willst" quickly catches the eye as out of place in an oft used Keller phrase. Originally the poem had read, "Tu frei und offen was du nicht kannst lassen" (XVI, 53), which was a wholehearted reaffirmation of Keller's belief in man's adherence to nature.

Man's arrayal in the natural order is also indicated in the poem "Abgedroschenes" of 1844:

> Eisern ans Schicksal der Menschheit gekettet,
> Hart in das Joch des Gesetzes gebettet,
> Jeder ein Hüter vom heiligen Schatz ...[17]

A diary notation of 1843 reveals to what an extent Keller's general thinking was influenced by his belief that man belonged to the natural order:

> Von Hoffmann zu verlangen, dasz er die Malerei aufgeben und alle seine Kräfte der Dichtkunst zuwenden solle, wäre eine Philisterei gewesen ... Aber es ist ein frommer Wunsch, dasz er diesen Drang zur Bildnerei nicht gehabt. (*Ermatinger* II, 107)

An indirect indication that man belonged in the natural order is seen in a poem of 1844 in which nations are conceived in terms of organic life:

> Wenn aus der Völker Schwellen und Versanden
> Ein Neues sich zum Ganzen einreiht ...
> (XIV, 76, *Vaterländische Sonette*)

Man's destiny, Keller felt, was especially guided by the law of time. With the philosophic optimism of the preceding century,

---

[17] XIII, 101. The demand in the second stanza of this poem, "Aber der Geist soll fessellos schweben," may be taken to be a defense of a Kantian or romantic dualism. If so, it would indicate a momentary yielding to the pressing philosophic arguments of the romantic group surrounding Keller. *Geist* may also be translated as "intellect," however, and then the poem fits in perfectly with the thesis of intellectual freedom as here developed.

Keller believed that man was evolving, inevitably driven by natural law, to perfection. Already in Munich in 1841 he had felt the deep significance of the passage of time:

> Die Zeit kommt her, die Zeit geht hin,
> Sie heilet alle Wunden . . .

In 1843, when he joined the fight against the Jesuits, it was his faith in inevitable progress that enabled him to defy his opponents:

> Die Zeit ist Gott! Und wenn ihr seine Zeichen
> Nicht achten wollet in verstockten Herzen,
> Wenn ihr der klaren Ueberzeugung nicht wollt weichen,
> So grabt ihr in der eigenen Brust nach bittern Schmerzen,
> . . .
> Wer frevelnd sich dem Rad der Zeit entgegenstemmt,
> Der liegt zerquetscht, zermalmt von der Riesenwucht.
> Vergeblich, dasz ihr seine ehrnen Speichen hemmt!
> Es rollet über euch dahin in rascher Flut.
> (XIII, 182)

The inevitable march of time was the basis of the nature experience contained in "Morgenlied" written a month later:

> Auch durch Gewitterstunden die Zeit entflieht
> Mit aller Not und Klage dahin sie zieht!
> (XIII, 40)

A *Zeitgedicht* of 1844 again revealed optimistic faith in the future based on the idea of inevitable progress:

> Wenn der kalte Winter nicht wäre
> Könnte uns nicht der Lenz beglücken!
> Wenn es keine Tyrannen gäbe
> Hätten wir keine Republiken!
>
> Alles musz keimen, reifen hienieden,
> Und die Zeit, die Zeit ist der Bauer,
> Der der Zukunft heiligen Samen
> Lockt aus dem dunklen Acker der Trauer.
> . . . Endlich wird doch Vollendung werden,
> Einzig Ziel von Sterben und Leben.
> (XIII, 226)

Other poems of 1844 develop the same theme and show how deeply rooted these convictions were in Keller's outlook:

THE BASIC CONCEPTS, 1837-1849

> Und magst du immer schlafen gehen,
> Die Sonne wird nicht stille stehen,
> Die Zeit wird nicht erfrieren!
> Und wann er schläft, der faule Rat,
> So steht sie auf, die frische Tat,
> Und wird den Reigen führen!
> (XIII, 276)

> Geduld ihr Hoffnungslosen,
> Die ihr glaubt zu erliegen!
> Die Zeit, die Zeit bringt Rosen,
> Sie wird auch für uns siegen.
> (XIII, 236)

In 1846 Keller was still proclaiming the same message:

> Unermüdlich schafft die Zeit
> Und wer sich mit ihr entzweit,
> Heimlich und am Tage,
> Tut es sich zur Plage!
> (XIII, 307)

A notation in his diary of 1848 read as follows:

> Und ebenso still, grosz und sicher leuchtet das
> Gestirn unseres Schicksals und unserer Tage über
> der tosenden Verwirrung.
> (*Ermatinger* II, 168)

A benign reason was inexorably guiding the destiny of man through the confusion of the times. Till 1848, then, man also was a part of the great natural order.

A concrete answer to the question of what Keller's views were on immortality and the relation of God to nature is somewhat more difficult to give because Keller's conception of immortality changed through the early forties and because his vehement defense of God and immortality during the years 1846-1848 was by no means the certain expression of his own convictions. Keller had defended the liberal, religious point of view against the atheist-philosopher Arnold Ruge in 1846 and then later against the Feuerbach disciple Wilhelm Marr, but it is quite possible that he was merely repaying a debt to his benefactor, Follen. Dünnebier realized this possibility although he then rejected it:

> Die Frage, ob Kellers Haltung im Ichelkampf von seinen Dankes-
> gefühlen für Follen geboten sei, darf man getrost mit dem Hin-
> weis auf seine selbständige religiöse Ueberzeugung verneinen, doch
> würde er ohne die Freunde Follen und Schulz schwerlich sich an
> den Streitigkeiten beteiligt haben (*op. cit.* p. 42).

It is undeniable, however, that Follen, as Ruge wrote to his friend Prutz in January 1846, put pressure on Keller to get him to support his own diatribe, *An die gottlosen Nichts-Wüteriche*:

> Wenn Follen es dahin bringt, dasz ihm einer eine populäre Philip-
> pika gegen die Philosophie und gegen mich speziell fabrizierte (er
> sucht den Gottfried Keller, einen guten, unbefangenen Kerl dazu
> zu bringen, wahrscheinlich ohne Erfolg) so wäre ich die längste
> Zeit hier Abt gewesen. (*Ermatinger* I, 160.)

Undeniable also, that immortality as represented in Keller's philippic, "Auch an die Ichel" (1846), would imply a retrogression in his thought:

> Was aber ward und wird aus den Millionen
> Die unversöhnt, bleich, siech von hinnen schwinden?
> Wie pitoyabel euer Lichtlein glimmt!

This proof of immortality, that millions die without reaching perfection, would imply that human spirits retain their identity after death to continue a monad-like development toward perfection. Even Dünnebier, with his emphasis on the change wrought by Feuerbach, admitted that by 1845 or earlier, Keller had no longer believed in personal immortality:

> Beide Gedichte stammen aus dem Jahre 1845, die Keime zu diesem
> Pantheismus mögen aber in einer früheren Schicht liegen, denn
> an eine Fortdauer des Menschen als P e r s o n hat der junge
> Keller, nachdem ihn einmal religiöse Dinge ernsthaft bewegten,
> kaum je geglaubt, obwohl er ... den Unsterblichkeitsglauben noch
> 1848 mit Leidenschaft verteidigt. (*op. cit.*, p. 30)

Furthermore, the oft-cited philosophic agreement between Follen and Keller may be opened to question in the light of Keller's reaction to Follen's revision of his poems.[18] The religious ideas in Keller's polemic writings of 1846-1848 are thus unreliable sign-posts. If they do reveal a sincere belief in God and immortality, there still is the question whether Keller conceived of them as stated and whether he felt as sure of himself on the subject as the writings would indicate. Fortunately, Keller's writ-

---

[18] Cf. pp. 24 and 53 in this study.

ings prior to 1846, though few, are more helpful and here one finds facts to indicate that long before 1849, indeed as early as 1845, God and nature had drawn very close together in Kellers outlook in the *Ruhe* common to both, and that personal immortality had been surrendered in favor of the more consistent pantheistic belief that death implied a return to the great eternal *Ruhe* which was god-nature.[19]

To begin with, Keller had a deep, innate preference for quiet moods. His *Traumbuch* and diary reveal this predilection:

> Nun stellte sie eine Nelke nach der andern bedächtig in das schlanke, glänzende Glas, ich sah ihr zu und empfand jenes Behagen und Wohlgefühl, welches immer in einen kömmt, wenn jemand vor unsern Augen eine leichte Arbeit still, ruhig, und zierlich vollbringt. (*Ermatinger*, II, 160. *Traumbuch*, 1847)

> Aber nicht blosz in Tagen der Mutlosigkeit—nein, auch in Tagen der festlichen, rauschenden Freude will ich stille Momente verweilen und ausruhen im traulichen Schmollwinkel meines Tagesbuches. (*Ermatinger*, II, 104. *Tagebuch*, 1843)

> Wenn ich auch nichts Lesenswertes mehr in dem Aufgeschriebenen finde, so wird mich doch beim Anblick der jeweiligen Daten eine dunkle, süsze Erinnerung befallen eines still genossenen, schuldlosen Glückes. (*Ermatinger* II, 161. *Tagebuch*, 1848)

His love for quiet and seclusion manifested itself in a liking for the quiet moods in nature. The letter of 1837 had called for "ein ruhiges Anschauen der Natur" with the obvious implication that a turbulent state of mind could not appreciate the peaceful wonder of nature. The essay of 1837, *Eine Nacht auf dem Uto*, contained a description of a sunset which had ended with the enraptured exclamation, "welch heilige Stille!" The little poem of 1838, "Beim Entwurf einer kleinen Landschaft," was the first of numerous lyrics dealing with quiet nature moods:

> Die Abendröte malet
> Schon See und Flur und Hain:
> Das ew'ge Lichtlein strahlet
> Still vom Kapellelein.
> Es strahlt so sanft,
> Es strahlt so mild,
> Als wärs der ew'gen Treue Bild
> Als wärs das Bild der Liebe.
> (XIII, 3)

---

[19] Hans Dünnebier believed that Keller's ideas on *Ruhe* were borrowed from Ludwig Feuerbach in 1849 (*op. cit.*, p. 74).

The peace of dawn, the silent glory of the sunset, the deep rest of night, the quiet of a winter morning, the noon-day hush in summer: these were the moments in nature which Keller preferred and which he depicted over and over again.

Keller's aesthetic experience in the quiet of nature was apparently so great that he objectivized his experience and considered nature's real essence to be peace and quiet, or *Ruhe*. The philosophic poem of 1838, "Misztraue Allem Auszerordentlichen," considered nature to be essentially at rest: "so einfach still zu sein wie die Natur." Young Heinrich substantiated this view of nature as essentially "still":

> Sie (die Landschaftsmalerei) besteht nicht darin, dasz man merkwürdige und berühmte Orte aufsucht und nachahmt, sondern darin, dasz man die stille Herrlichkeit und Schönheit der Natur betrachtet und abzubilden sucht . . . (XVII, 46)

Heinrich also associated "Gottes freie Natur" with scenes representing nature at rest:

> In den Städten, in den Häusern der Vornehmen, da hängen schöne, glänzende Gemälde, welche meistens stille, grüne Wildnisse vorstellen, so reizend und trefflich gemalt, als sähe man in Gottes freie Natur. (XVII, 46)

The poems of the *Nachtzyklus* already have shown that Keller's aesthetic experience in the peace of nature at night became an intense religious experience. Then he felt close to God and at peace with the world:

> Doch wie nun auf dem Erdental
> Ein absolutes Schweigen ruht:
> Ich fühle mich so leicht zumal
> Und wie die Welt so still und gut.
>   (XIV, 29)
>
> Hier fühl ich Zusammenhang
> Mit dem All und Einen!
>   (XIV, 30)

Just as he had objectivized his general aesthetic experience in nature, he now lent objective validity to his profound religious experience in nature. A poem of 1844 began, "Gott ist ein groszes stilles Haus." The fifteen-year-old Heinrich (after having read Goethe, to be sure) came to the conclusion:

> Nur die Ruhe in der Bewegung hält die Welt und macht den Mann; die Welt ist innerlich ruhig und still, und so musz es auch der Mann

> sein, der sie verstehen und als ein wirkender Teil von ihr sie
> wiederspiegeln will. Ruhe zieht das Leben an, Unruhe verscheucht
> es; Gott hält sich mäuschen still, darum bewegt sich die Welt
> um ihn. (XVIII, 6)

God was "mäuschen still." It will also be noticed that though God is still viewed as an entity, there is almost an identification of the inner peace of the world with God, since in the last line the world is moving about God, and before that, it was said that the world was inwardly at rest. Thus, the sparse references available indicate that Keller associated both nature and God with *Ruhe* before 1849.

It would seem that just about the time Keller came to conceive of God in pantheistic terms as *Ruhe* in nature, he also surrendered his belief in personal immortality. The manner in which immortality is viewed strongly colors one's conception of death, and conversely a new conception of death almost inevitably implies a change in one's view of the after-life. Such a new conception of death was revealed in "Wetternacht" (1845).[20] The poem begins with a description of a cold and stormy night; the poet is seized by the tremendous sadness in nature:

> Es weint das tiefverhüllte Land.
> In meinem Herzen tönt die Klage wieder.
> Und es ergreift mich, wirft zum Staub mich nieder,
> Und meine Tränen rinnen in den Sand.
> (XIV, 25-27)

In this mood of humility, the poet's pride is broken, and he sees for the first time into the deepest recesses of nature:

> O reiner Schmerz, der in den Höhen gewittert,
> Du heil'ges Weh, das durch die Tiefen zittert,
> Ihr schloszt auch mir die Augen auf!
> Ihr habt zu mir das Zauberwort gesprochen,
> Und meinen Hochmut wie ein Rohr gebrochen,
> Und ungehemmt strömt meiner Tränen Lauf.
> Du süszes Leid hast ganz mich überwunden!
> Welch dunkle Lust, die ich noch nie empfunden,
> Ist glühend in mir angefacht!
> Wie reich bist Mutter Erde! du zu nennen:
> Ich glaubte deine Herrlichkeit zu kennen,
> Nun erst schau ich in deinen tiefsten Schacht.

---

[20] *Wetternacht* has generally been ignored by Keller critics, though Hans Corrodi noted that it reflected sincere inner experience and had been unjustifiedly overlooked. (*Gottfried Keller's Weltanschauung, Zeitwende*, Dec., 1932). A similar attitude is to be found in "Abendlied an die Natur" (1845).

Out of the shaft comes death, "ein junger, schlanker Knabe," whom the poet welcomes:

> Willkommen Tod! dir will ich mich vertrauen.
> Lasz mich in deine treuen Augen schauen
> Zum ersten Male fest und klar.

For the first time the poet has realized the true nature of death, and he returns to life filled with a new "Todesdemut":

> Der Welt mit Weltsinn nun entgegen gehen
> Will ich, doch innen blüht mir ungesehen
> Der Todesdemut still verborgner Glanz.

To understand the full significance of the poem one must analyze the key to its meaning, namely, the poet's pride. Only when his pride is finally broken by the intense sadness in nature, does he see, for the first time, into nature's greatest mystery. Now, there was only one thing which Keller might at this time have regarded as pride in the presence of nature, a belief in personal immortality which defied the laws of nature; for only as long as the human soul was considered apart from nature, could death not be understood in terms of nature. Keller had long concerned himself with the problem of death and immortality and the two were constantly related in his mind. After the death of Henriette Keller in 1838 he had pondered the matter more deeply than ever. A month before writing "Wetternacht," he had conceived of death in semi-pantheistic terms, man returning to the vast sea of life. Speaking of a dead child, he says:

> Zu der du wiederkehrst, grüsz mir die Quelle
> Des Lebens Born, doch besser; grüsz mir das Meer,
> Das eine Meer des Lebens, dessen Welle
> Hoch flutet um die dunkle Klippe her,
> Darauf er sitzt, der traurige Geselle,
> Der Tod—verlassen, einsam, tränenschwer,
> Wenn ihm die frohen Seelen, kaum gefangen,
> Mit lautem Jubel wieder auf die See gegangen.
>   (XIV, 278)

"Bei einer Kindesleiche" did not really surrender the conventional notion of immortality, however. The child, though it went out on the sea of life, did not become merged with the sea, but retained its identity. Furthermore, the souls who *escaped* death still viewed him as an unpleasant fellow whom they were glad to be rid of. In "Wetternacht," on the other hand, the profound nature experience apparently made the poet realize that he, body and soul, belonged to nature, and that the stubborn retention of his superiority in asserting personal immortality was foolish pride. For now death was revealed to him as something entirely new: one of *nature's* mysteries and kind and good. To be sure, the goodness of death in itself might be a eulogy to personal immortality like that voiced in "Auch an die Ichel," but the emphasis on death as *nature's* secret cannot mean other than that death meant a return to "Mutter Erde." And since God was becoming identified with nature in Keller's pantheistic outlook,[21] any interpretation that death was a portal to God would mean the same thing as a return to nature. In view of the fact, furthermore, that Keller thought of nature as essentially "still" (so still zu sein wie die Natur), death would appear to mean a return to rest in nature and immortality would seem to approximate deep, dreamless sleep.[22] The logical development of such an interpretation of death as a return to rest in nature is seen in "Der Alte Bettler" (1848):

> O gute Scholle meiner Heimaterde,
> Wie kriech ich gern in deinen warmen Schosz,
> Mir ahnet schon, wie sanft ich ruhen werde,
> Vom Kaun des Brotes und allem Irrsal los.
>   (XVi, 106)

To sum up our discussion of *Natur* during Keller's early period, then, it has been shown that *Natur* represented the world of tangible objects and the divinely purposeful laws by which they were governed. God and nature were both associated with the idea of *Ruhe* and so with each other. Man was considered an integral part of nature, subservient to all her laws, for whom, after 1845, death meant a peaceful, impersonalized return to rest in God-nature. *Natur* implied a cosmos which was a dynamic monism, and a philosophy similar to the pantheism of Herder.

---

[21] Dünnebier agreed that by 1844 Keller had a pantheistic conception of God. Speaking of the poem, "Gott ist ein groszes, stilles Haus," he said: "Mit der pantheistischen Gottesauffassung, wie sie sich klar in den angeführten Strophen ausspricht, gehört Keller sowieso in seiner (Schleiermachers) Nähe. (*Op. cit.*, p. 23.)

[22] Dünnebier agreed that Keller's immortality was not personal, though he felt Feuerbach gave Keller his conception of reality as *Ruhe*. (Cf. p. 28 above.)

B. *Freiheit*

Natur, as used in the second passage from the letter of 1837, could awaken a divine freedom in man. What was this freedom, which was neither license (des Pöbels) nor political freedom, and which required that one consciously seek to fit oneself into the natural order?

As *Freiheit* "permitted of no evil conduct," it is apparent that the concept referred to is abstruse; obviously, if one's pattern of conduct is prescribed in advance, there is no practical freedom present. Such concepts of limited or hypothetical freedom are common enough in philosophy and are particularly evident in the thinking of the German philosophers. Leibniz, for example, conceived of freewill in his pre-established harmony by viewing a free act as one which was in accordance with man's inner nature; although God in his infinite wisdom had predetermined the act by creating a particular type of individual, the latter acted freely in carrying out the act according to his inner need.[23] Kant justified a freewill which did not violate the law of cause and effect in nature, by postulating a dualistic universe.[24]

The definition of *Freiheit* given by Keller in the second passage permits at first glance of a number of possible interpretations, and since the concept is of crucial importance to our study, we shall consider each interpretation in turn. First, it will be well to presume with Hans Dünnebier that *Freiheit* meant absolute freewill, which in a monistic world is equivalent to freedom of action.

Dünnebier referred to the young Keller's conception of *Freiheit* as an "unumschränkte Geist der Freiheit."[25] Such a view appears plausible enough at the outset since in the second passage of the letter man was endowed with God's freedom (" . . . die Gott selbst eigen ist"), and any doubt as to whether Keller meant God's freedom in a literal sense would seem dispelled by the fact that he imbued the young Grüne Heinrich with a somewhat similar view some thirteen years later:[26]

> Ebenso betrachte ich die Welt der Geister als eine Republik, die nur Gott als Protektor über sich habe, dessen Majestät in voll-

---
[23] Gottfried Wilhelm Leibniz: *New Essays Concerning Human Understanding*.
[24] Immanuel Kant: *Kritik der reinen Vernunft*.
[25] Dünnebier: *op. cit.*, p. 74.
[26] Cf. fn. 9.

kommener Freiheit das Gesetz heilig hielte, das er gegeben, und diese Freiheit sei auch unsere Freiheit und unsere Freiheit die Seinige. (XVII, 206)

In Heinrich's mind the freedom of God was absolute and man's freedom should be the same. Man should obey the divine law, apparently not through compulsion but rather from a sense of moral obligation, patently on the grounds that natural law reflected the will of the Great Creator to whom man had reason to be so profoundly grateful and whom he knew to be so infinitely wise and good. A feeling of such moral obligation is apparent in Heinrich's statement:

> Die moralische Wichtigkeit dieses Unabhängigkeitssinnes scheine mir sehr grosz und gröszer zu sein, als wir es uns vielleicht denken können. (XVII, 206)

Thus, if one is ready to identify young Heinrich's conception of *Freiheit* with that of the young Keller, it might appear that *Freiheit* as used in the second passage referred to an absolute freewill.

But let us investigate this interpretation further and see how it stands up in the light of the other definitive characteristics of *Freiheit*. It will be remembered, for example, that the possession of *Freiheit* permitted of no evil deed. How can this moral compulsion be explained where there is only moral obligation?

From a philosophical point of view this apparent paradox does not present too difficult a problem. In the letter of 1837, Keller had voiced his belief that man's natural inclination was essentially moral: "Der Mensch soll nicht tugendhaft sondern nur natürlich sein, und die Tugend wird von selbst kommen." Once free, man in his goodness would apparently not want to do wrong. Man would be somewhat like the deistic God referred to by Heinrich, who obeyed his own laws voluntarily. The conventional deistic argument which explains God's obedience to his own laws goes as follows: God, though absolute, had to obey the laws he had created as they were the complete expression of his will; God, though completely free, was unable to violate the law since his every act was bound to conform to the law which was the expression of his will. All this simply means that God acted freely but in accordance with his nature and it follows that man, too, might be assumed to be absolutely free and yet restricted in similar fashion by the goodness of his nature.

A real weakness in this interpretation of *Freiheit*, however, is that it does not show why man in his inherent goodness did not always act morally *even before* he was aware of his freedom. Since recognition of freewill was of key-importance, it would appear that some recognitional freedom was prerequisite to moral action.

The basic weakness of the interpretation is its inability to explain why man felt "a mighty sensation of freedom" only after he realized that he belonged to nature where everything was completely regulated and unfree. By stretching the imagination, one might reason in terms of Herder's evolutionary philosophy that only a consciousness of one's relation to nature could make one aware that man was the end-product of nature, the favorite of God, and endowed with God's own attributes of intellect and freedom. It would seem, however, that to seek one's destiny in the realm of natural law ("das seine Bestimmung aufsucht in der Welten harmonischer Wechselbewegung") would indicate far rather an adherence to natural law than a freedom from it. Thus, absolute freewill or freedom of action as the meaning of *Freiheit* leads to too many contradictions to warrant its unqualified acceptance.

Another interpretation of *Freiheit* is suggested if emphasis is removed from its divine nature and placed on the fact that only when a person belonged to nature and himself was he filled with a "divine sense of natural justice and a mighty sensation of freedom." Such a paradoxical view, in which an adherence to nature—nature is identified with "der Welten harmonischer Wechselbewegung"—awakens a mighty sense of freedom, may be understood as proceeding from the emotional experience of a person who has just substituted a deistic for a theologic *Weltanschauung*. As long as he believes in a personal God who watches over his every move, he has no freedom. But when he realizes that he is subject to the immutable laws of nature and is thus free from intervention by a personal God, he becomes filled with a sensation of freedom. His God changes from a despot to Heinrich's republican "protector," and his world from a benevolent despotism to a republic in which he is free within the frame-work of natural law. But now just what does this mean? One cannot assume the logical corollary that violation of the law involved punishment as in a republic, since a belief that man did good to avoid punishment was far too utilitarian for the idealistic young Keller. Even in later years Keller derided utilitarian ethical systems.[27] If one is to assume, however, that man obeyed the law merely because in his inherent goodness he so desired, the whole discussion is reduced to a variation of the first interpretation of *Freiheit* as freedom of action. On the other hand, the assumption that man had to obey the law with no choice whatever would apparently rule out all freedom and would lead to the absurd conclusion that the young Keller was a full-fledged determinist. Only one possibility is left: man was free not to violate the law, but to choose which law he wanted to obey. Here, in the choice between two inviolable courses of action, there is no longer any real freedom of action but rather a recognitional freedom of a nature now to be discussed.

The most feasible explanation of *Freiheit* is, then, that it referred to the recognitional freedom to discern right from wrong, not unlike the moral freedom of the German Idealists (although with no implication of a dualistic world, as Keller definitely said that to acquire freedom man had to belong to nature and had to seek his destiny in the world of cause and effect). Such a restricted freedom allows, first of all, for the most logical explanation of why man had to belong to nature. His adherence to nature made him realize that he was subservient to natural law, and that he, like the other creatures in nature, had a prescribed course to follow. Since the latter obeyed the law by heeding their innate urge, man had only to do likewise. And since the natural law was the expression of God's will, acts based on inner necessity were moral. The validity of this line of reasoning is confirmed by the identification of "virtuous" and "natural" in the sentence already quoted from the letter of 1837: "Der Mensch soll nicht tugendhaft sondern nur natürlich sein, und die Tugend wird von selbst kommen."

This interpretation also affords an adequate explanation of why the knowledge of *Freiheit* could only be acquired by "der

---

[27] Keller often voiced disapproval of the Christian ethic for the utilitarianism implicit in the doctrine "der Glaube macht selig" and felt that such *Glaube* was far removed from the true faith and from a true understanding of the Providence which "geht gleich einem Stern im Himmel . . ." (XVII, 204). In a letter of 1856 Keller stated explicitly what had been implicit in many of his anti-ecclesiastical remarks before 1849: "Es gibt gewisz keine ärgere Utilitätstheorie als das Christentum predigt" (*Ermatinger*, II, 424).

Mensch, der der Natur *und sich selbst* angehört"[28] and by "ein reines, denkendes Herz, das seine Bestimmung aufsucht in der Welten harmonischer Wechselbewegung." Only a person who realized his adherence to nature, only a sincere thinker who sought his place in the natural order would be able to shake himself free of conventional preconceptions sufficiently to understand the true nature of man. Not until then could he know that moral action meant natural and necessary action.

The "mighty sensation of freedom" experienced by a man who is aware of his adherence to nature can be adequately explained as a realization of *moral* freedom. Such a man knew that he could be himself in the fullest sense of the word and still be moral. Obedience to God's law did not require an abnegation of self. There was no conflict between the laws governing man and the deep inner drive of one's nature.

The fact that *Freiheit* "did not let him who acquired it do an evil deed" follows simply enough. Until man became fully enlightened, he was liable to misinterpret his inner need and do evil. Only when he understood himself could he always interpret his inner urge correctly. There is here no hint of free *action* since free man had also to heed his inner need, but was able to do so in such a way that necessary, moral action resulted.[29]

As for the identification of man's freedom with God's freedom,[30] it can be explained in terms of the deistic interpretation given above wherein God's action was restricted to moral action because of the necessary identity of God's will and natural law. Man's freedom is similar to God's in that man's also involves an identity of individual will and natural law. God in his great wisdom fitted man along with the other creatures of the world into the great natural order so that man's inner urge was a direct expression of divine omnipotence and natural law. Both man and God, acting in complete freedom, i.e., in strict accord with their true, inner desire, obeyed the law.

What now is the precise nature of this recognitional freedom? Clearly, it contains two elements: 1) the intellectual clarity which enabled man to perceive his true nature and his relation to natural law; 2) the moral discernment to interpret one's in-

---

[28] My italics.
[29] Keller in his later life would never admit to a principle of evil. Wickedness was always due to ignorance and misunderstanding. Cf. p. 95 ff.
[30] Cf. fn. 9.

ner urge correctly. *Freiheit* may thus be defined as moral freedom based on enlightenment. It is close in meaning, though with Keller's peculiar implications, to the German term *Geistesfreiheit* and, for the sake of fluency, will occasionally be translated as "intellectual freedom."

In the years that followed, Keller became so intensely interested in the means to moral freedom, namely enlightenment, that often he seemed to refer solely to that aspect of *Freiheit*. However, the fact that he always associated happiness and justice with the idea of universal *Freiheit* reveals that moral freedom was always implicitly present in the concept as well.

So much attention has been given to the letter of 1837 because it contained the ideas which were to form the basis of his mature *Weltanschauung*, ideas which have been attributed by many outstanding Keller scholars to the influence of Feuerbach.[31] Now, to show the logical development of *Freiheit* throughout Keller's early period and to diminish further the philosophical importance of Feuerbach for Keller, let us consider that concept in Keller's writings from 1837 to 1849.

It is not probable that Keller was fully conscious of all the implications, nor reasoned as minutely as we have done above, in the development of his idea of *Freiheit*, since he was not trained in or particularly adapted to speculative thinking. In fact, it is more than likely, as we shall see later, that he borrowed the concept from another writer. The important thing for our purposes is, however, that unconsciously or otherwise, the concept of *Freiheit* as developed above was in his mind. This fact is apparent from a diary passage of 1838 in which he shows the same deep interest in "intellectual independence":

> Ein Mann ohne Tagebuch . . . ist was ein Weib ohne Spiegel. Dieses hört auf ein Weib zu sein, wenn es nicht mehr zu gefallen strebt und seine Anmut vernachlässigt; es wird seiner Bestimmung dem Manne gegenüber untreu. Jener hört auf ein Mann zu sein, wenn er sich selbst nicht mehr beobachtet, und Erholung und Nahrung auszer sich sucht. Er verliert seine Haltung, seine Festigkeit, seinen Charakter, und wenn er seine geistige Seltständigkeit dahin gibt, so wird er ein Tropf. Diese Selbständigkeit kann aber nur bewahrt werden durch stetes Nachdenken über sich selbst. (*Ermatinger* II, 101)

---

[31] Cf. the discussion of Ermatinger and Dünnebier, app., pp. 144-147.

A superficial reading of this passage might lead one to believe that Keller had subordinated moral integrity to intellectual clarity as *Charakter* is relinquished more readily than *Geistige Selbständigkeit*. A closer study, however, shows that *Charakter* is used here rather loosely as a middle stage between outer mannerliness (*Haltung*) and inner moral discernment, and that the entire passage is primarily concerned with the preservation of moral integrity. Keller was thinking in terms of the moral degeneration undergone by a person who constantly wants to be entertained and is unwilling to do any serious thinking about his relation to life. Such a person, he felt, deteriorated first outwardly, losing his *Haltung*, and then inwardly, the decay spreading to include *Festigkeit* and *Charakter*. Finally, if no preventive steps were taken, the person lost his *geistige Selbständigkeit*. Why was the latter loss so vital? Because *geistige Selbständigkeit*, inasmuch as it could be safe-guarded by diligent self-observation,[32] referred to the intellectual clarity which enabled one to perceive his own true nature and thus, in the light of what has already been shown regarding enlightenment, referred by implication to moral freedom. Certainly, the moral aspect of *geistige Selbständigkeit* is apparent from the fact that *geistige Selbständigkeit, Festigkeit* and *Charakter* were all safe-guarded by introspection (" . . . wenn er sich nicht mehr beobachtet . . . verliert er seine Festigkeit, seinen Charakter . . . diese Selbständigkeit kann aber nur bewahrt werden durch stetes Nachdenken über sich selbst"). The significance of knowing oneself was that it enabled man to act according to his inner nature, to be himself, to be moral, and to avoid what Keller hated and derided in later life more than anything else, to be "eine Abirrung von sich selbst." Thus, "intellectual independence" contains both the elements of enlightenment and moral freedom and is comparable to the concept of intellectual freedom.

The importance placed by Keller on enlightenment as the means to moral freedom presupposes a fervent striving toward truth, so that it is not surprising to find the toast in a student

---

[32] This intense, early interest on Keller's part in self-observation should be kept in mind in view of the general belief, voiced by Dünnebier and other scholars, that Keller had derived his conception of *Selbsterkenntnis* from Ludwig Feuerbach. Even the terminology was not new to Keller; poems later in the chapter will show this use of *Erkenntnis*. As will be shown to have been the case in most instances, Keller merely adopted with enthusiasm those elements of Feuerbach's philosophy which concurred with his own.

poem written while he was in Munich dedicated to "die freie Wahrheit":

> Dir, O Wahrheit soll es gelten!
> Freie Wahrheit streng und hart!
> (XIII, 14)

And, when the issue of the reintroduction of the Jesuit order into Switzerland arose in 1843, it was the same veneration of intellectual clarity that made Keller a bitter opponent of the plan. True, he had never been unduly sympathetic with religion as a whole, but he had never broken completely with orthodox Christianity, which had remained despite everything "eine so schöne, zarte Sache."[33] The Jesuits, however, stood, in Keller's eyes, for repressive dogma,[34] and he declared that he would rather "keinen Glauben herrschend wissen, als den schwarzen, keuchenden, ertötenden Glaubenszwang." Whereupon he issued a declaration of war:

> Ich werfe mich dem Kampfe für völlige Unabhängigkeit und Freiheit des Geistes und der religiösen Ansichten in die Arme. (*Ermatinger* II, 114, 1843)

Three days later he repeated his declaration as a poet:

> Der Dichter aber musz ein positives Element, eine Religion haben. Gerade aber, weil er Dichter ist, so sollen seine religiösen Bedürfnisse frei von aller Form und allem Zwang sein, und er musz für diese Freiheit kämpfen. (*Ermatinger* II, 117)

---

[33] *Ermatinger* II, 115.
[34] Keller directed his most powerful attacks against the Jesuits. A few lines from one of his anti-Jesuit poems, "Jesuitenlied," will give an idea of his feeling:

> Huh! wie das krabbelt, kneipt und kriecht!
> Und wie's so infernalisch riecht!
> Jetzt fahre hin, du gute Ruh!
> Geh, Grete, mach das Fenster zu!
> Sie kommen, die Jesuiten!
>
> Von Kreuz und Fahne angeführt.
> *Den Giftsack hinten aufgeschnürt.*
> *Der Fanatismus als Profosz,*
> *Die Dummheit folgt als Betteltrosz:*
> Sie kommen, die Jesuiten!
>
> O Schweizerland, du schöne Braut,
> Du bist dem Teufel angetraut! ...
> Sie kommen, die Jesuiten!
> (XIV, 207, 1843) (my italics)

The Jesuit issue crystallized Keller's attitude and stirred him to action. From August, 1843, on, till the fight against Jesuits and aristocrats was won, Keller directed more than 150 fiery poems against these adversaries of freedom.[35] As it has not been generally realized that Keller's interest in *Freiheit* went deeper than political or religious freedom, it is well at this point to show the relative importance of these concepts for him.

Keller, like most Swiss, came early to believe in the right of political self-determination, and this belief was strengthened in him by his experiences in Munich, then the capital of a monarchy, and by his political affiliations in Zürich; the opinion he voiced in "Die Feier der deutschen Unabhängigkeit seit 843" (1843) was deep-seated:

> Was schieret uns ein freies Land
> Wenn die drin wohnen Knechte sind?
> (XIII, 188)

But political freedom alone he deemed insufficient. The theme of an essay of 1841, *Vermischte Gedanken über die Schweiz,* had been the need for intellectual clarity to preserve political freedom.[36] The more basic interest in enlightenment is also clear from several of the *Vaterländische Gedichte*:

> Ja, du bist frei, mein Volk, von Eisenketten
> Und von des Vorrechts unerhörter Schande,
> Kein Adel schmiegt dich in schnöde Bande
> Und fröhlich magst du dich im Wohlstand betten.
>
> Doch dies kann nicht dich vor der Knechtschaft retten
> Der schwarzen, die im weiszen Schafsgewande . . .
> Wenn du nicht kühnlich magst den Geist entbinden
> Von allem Schwulst und tödtender Umhüllung . . .
> (XIV, 77, 1843)

> Weiszt du warum du büszen
> Mein Vaterland und leiden muszt?
> Du hast der Freiheit Gaben
> Verkannt und unnütz angewandt!
> Du hast dein Schwert geschwungen
> Weh! für des Fleisches Freiheit nur!
> Der Geist, der blieb gezwungen
> Und öde seine Spur!   (XIII, 269, 1844)

---

[35] Keller's political poetry of the years 1843-1849 in its entirety is only available in the Fränkel edition, Volumes XIII and XIV (*Nachgelassene Gedichte*). Fränkel published the lyrics in their *original* form, not as printed in the *Gesammelte Gedichte* which contained the poems as revised by Follen. Included in this edition are also copious notes.

[36] Cf. p. 133 in this study.

Practically all of Keller's "political" poems show this emphasis on freedom of the intellect rather than on personal liberty. In the political poem *Aufruf*, freedom was to guide its followers through the pitfalls that beset the mind:

> Die Freiheit unser Grundton ist,
> Den wollen wir fest halten!
> Er leite uns zu jeder Frist
> Durch Irrtum, Falschheit, Trug und List
> Und finstre Wut der Alten!
> (XIII, 171)

A *Zeitgedicht* of 1843 offered double praise for the enlightened individual who fought in defense of ideals:

> Heil dem, der ehrlich sagen kann:
> "Auch ich hab mitgestritten!"
> Und zweifach Heil dem freien Mann,
> Der für das Wort gelitten!
> (XIII, 173)

Another *Zeitgedicht* of 1843 identified freedom with light, an obvious symbolism:

> Sollen wir für Licht und Freiheit rechten,
> Lasz allein, O Herr, den Kampf uns fechten!
> Wollen gründlich wir uns einst befreien
> Musz die Ehr erleuchten unsre Reihen.
> (XIII, 178)

The last two lines of the poem "Von Kindern" show Keller's interest in freedom as an *element of attitude*:

> Mich kränken minder diese Herrschertriebe
> Als solchen Knechtsinns zeitiges Vollenden;
> (XV-1, 47)

A poem of 1844 revealed that *Freiheit* was a very general human ideal for which people everywhere had fought:

> Es ist auf Erden keine Statt
> Es ist kein Dorf, des stille Hut
> Nicht einen alten Kirchhof hat
> Drin ein Märtyr der Freiheit ruht.
> (XIV, 52)

Freedom from prejudice, misconception, and dogma, then, was more important to Keller than political freedom. To demonstrate now that *Freiheit* went deeper than *religiöse Gedankenfreiheit* is somewhat more difficult since freedom from dogma is after all enlightenment in reverse, and Keller often failed to make clear that full enlightenment implied moral freedom as well. One can of course refer to the fact that Keller's interest in enlightenment was active long before the outbreak of the politico-religious controversy in Switzerland and that this interest had always been for the sake of the related moral discernment. In the poems themselves, however, there is only one clue to indicate that *Freiheit* implied the positive freedom to act morally. This clue is the universal happiness, peace, justice, or other moral state, often associated with *Freiheit*, which could only be obtained under conditions of moral freedom. In a sonnet of 1846 *Freiheit* is associated with the millennium:

> Und wenn auch einst die Freiheit ist errungen,
> Die Menschheit hoch wie eine Rose blüht,
> Auch nicht vom kleinsten Dorne mehr umschlungen . . .
> (XIV, 89)

In "Pfingstfest" (1843) "certain recognition" was to bring a "beautiful cloudless day" to mankind:

> Befreiung sollte einst dem Erdensohn
> Der heilige Geist von seinen Fesseln bringen . . .
> O Herr! O Herr! wann sendest du den Tag,
> Der alle Völker wird mit Feuer taufen?
> Den unbewölkten, morgenklaren Tag,
> Durch den wir uns die Geistesfreiheit kaufen?
> Wann wird die dumpfe Glaubensangst sich wenden
> In freudigheitres, festes, sicheres Erkennen?
> (XIII, 314-315)

The "Geistesfreiheit" referred to in "Pfingstfest" is, to be sure, religious freedom—not mere freedom from dogma, however, but the intellectual and religious clarity which enabled one to perceive the true nature of God. Such positive religious freedom may be presumed to be identical with full enlightenment and to presuppose an understanding of the nature of the world as well. Certainly, the "beautiful, cloudless day" reveals that the Utopian state subsequent to universal enlightenment would then exist.

A poem of 1847 described an enlightened nation ("in der Freiheitsminne"), which recognized its nature, as "beautiful" and "victorious":

> Wie eine Braut am Hochzeitstage,
> So ist ein Volk, das sich erkennt . . .
> Wie schön sie sei, und fühlt es ganz:
> So stehet in der Freiheitsminne
> Ein Volk mit seinem Siegeskranz.
> (IIi, 68)

The deeply philosophical nature of the *Freiheit* which had become Keller's ideal is perhaps best revealed in the poem "Der Grüne Baum," which though included under the *Kampfsonette* is not a eulogy of political freedom, but a condensed personal history of the development of *Freiheit* in Keller's attitude.

> Ein brausend Gären und ein wildes Wogen,
> Ein zagend Raten und ein hilflos Irren,
> Ein *geistig* Banges schweres Kettenklirren—
> Sind mir die rauhen Tage hingezogen!
>
> Und stündlich neue Träume mich umflogen:
> Das war ein Leuchten, Blühen, Klingen, Schwirren,
> Das war ein stet Entwickeln und Verwirren,
> Und alles hat am Ende mir gelogen!
>
> (However, all of that was past for him now
> and out of the cemetery of his youthful
> erring, a tree has grown.)
>
> Der grüne Baum, er ist die gute Sache,
> Zu der ich nun vor aller Welt geschworen,
> Die teuere Freiheit, die ich mir erkoren
> Und zum Symbole meines Schildes mache.
>   (XIII, 149-150)   (my italics)

Throughout his youth he had constantly sought for clarity, had constantly been deceived, and finally after much heart-ache, had come to realize that *Freiheit* was of supreme importance. *Freiheit* as used here was more than political freedom or freedom from dogma. It was the result of a long search for a standard of human values and was a deeply philosophical concept. Thus, *Freiheit* would seem to refer to intellectual freedom, as that was the only philosophical freedom with which Keller was constantly concerned; and that such is actually the case will now be shown by considering the personal experiences referred to in the poem.

Keller was a very unhappy young man for a good part of the period 1837-1849. In 1838, he was undecided as to the choice of a profession. In the spring of that year occurred the death of Henriette Keller, whom he much admired. Ackerknecht summarized the youth's state of mind by heading the page discussing the events of that year: *Selbstquälerei*. The Munich years were filled with poverty and failure. With the return to Zürich came the bitter realization that he had caused his mother much suffering. In 1846 he fell in love again, deeply, probably with

Marie Melos, and though little of his feeling ever came to light and no proposal ensued, he nevertheless suffered another painful wound.

This continued misfortune gave an inclination to melancholy ample opportunity to come to expression—an inclination which was just as deeply rooted in Keller's personality as his indomitable optimism regarding the future. Whereas at first he had always envisaged *Glück* as success and happiness in the conventional sense, his melancholic brooding now occasionally led him to give up such dreams. At times he now sought refuge in philosophic resignation. Melancholy revealed to him the futility of life—though she then robbed him of even this consolation:

> . . .
> Die mir der Wahrheit Spiegel hält,
> Den düster blitzenden, empor,
> Dasz der Erkenntnis Träne schwellt,
> Und bricht aus zagem Aug hervor.
> . . . Es hängt mein Herz an eitler Lust
> Und an der Torheit dieser Welt:
> Oft mehr als eines Weibes Brust,
> Ist es von Auszenwerk umstellt!
> Und selbst den Trost, *dasz ich aus eignem Streben,*
> *Dasz Alles nichtig ist, erkannt,*
> Nimmst Du und hast mein stolz Erheben
> Zu Boden alsobald gewandt . . .
>   (XVi, 93)   (my italics)

After a while, however, the pendulum would swing back again, and his optimistic faith in the goodness and purposefulness of nature would reassert itself. Though he might brood and be unhappy, he could not alter the basic attitude which his nature experiences had given him. In the darkest of his Munich days he had ultimately imbued his tribulations with purposefulness and consoled himself that they were essential to the sound foundation which gave rise to the "Glück der späteren Tage." Likewise, in the middle 1840's, after he had experienced moods of depression, his optimism would reassert itself, and he came to view misfortune as good and purposeful. Misfortune shook one free of romantic illusions:

> Der Unglück ist der Wirbelwind
> Der peitscht uns bis wir schäumen
> Und bis wir wach geschlagen sind
> Von unsern Wasserträumen.
>   (XIV, 238) 1845

> Und aus dem Unglück nur entspringt das "Glück,
> Der Irrtum erst macht unser Leben ganz.
> (XIII, 93) 1843

> So grosz ist keines Unglücks Macht
> Ein Blümlein hängt in seiner Kette.
> (XIV, 14) 1844

Keller finally came to the conclusion that the real happiness in life was neither wealth nor success, but the acquisition of intellectual freedom. He expressed this idea neatly in a little formula found in his *Nachlasz*:

> Wert + Unglück = Bewusztsein = Glück (II 2, p. 223).

Misfortune brings to an essentially worthy person a consciousness which is in itself true happiness.

A different kind of personal experience which also tended to emphasize the importance of intellectual freedom was revealed in the poem "Wetternacht" discussed above. The fears and worries associated with the great mystery of death were dispelled by true understanding. Death was a friend, a part of nature's order. Armed with this new knowledge about himself the poet returned to the tasks of life with a greater peace of mind.

In his public life and in his most personal experiences, Keller remained constantly concerned with intellectual freedom. He became more and more convinced that prejudice, preconception, and misunderstanding were the root of all evil, and became increasingly certain that enlightenment was the sole panacea for man's ills. And with his optimistic faith in inevitable progress, his conviction became ever greater that the goal of mankind was precisely intellectual freedom. The eventual realization of *Freiheit* was assured in the purposefulness of the law of time:

> Frühlingszeit und Freiheitslust
> Und die Uhr in deiner Brust
> Sind nicht zu verdrehen.
> (XIII, 306)

> Und zischend hat des Todes Fluch
> Gelöscht der Freiheit Feuerspuren.
> Gelöscht? O nein! sie schlummert wohl.
> Die Zeit, die sie einst wecken soll,
> Schleicht fort auf der Geschichte Uhren.
> (XIII, 67)

> Ein Tannenbaum im Schwarzwald steht,
> Der wächst schon manches Jahr; . . .
> Doch alles was auf Erden ist
> Musz haben seine Zeit;
> Der Tannenbaum zu seiner Frist
> Zum Fällen ist bereit!
> O Maienlust, o Freiheitsbaum,
> So jugendlich und grün,
> Wie wirst du alter Menschentraum
> Dann ewig, ewig blühn.
>   (XIV, 218)

Nature had preordained that one day in the future, man would possess the "one, true, and pure freedom":

> Die Freiheit, einzig, rein, und wahr,
> Im Anfang schon beschlossen,
> Sie stellt sich endlich prangend dar,
> Von Siegesglanz umflossen.
>   (XIII, 175)

The final Utopia was to be a period of universal peace and enlightenment:

> Das ist das Lied vom Völkerfrieden
> Und von dem letzten Menschenglück,
> Von goldner Zeit, die einst hienieden
> Mit Glanz und Reinheit kehrt zurück;
>
> Wo einig alle Völker beten
> Zum einen König, Gott und Hirt . . .
>   (1844: XIV, 34)
>
> Und wenn auch einst die Freiheit ist errungen,
> Die Menschheit hoch wie eine Rose blüht
> Auch nicht vom kleinsten Dorne mehr umschlungen . . .
>   (XIV, 89)

That the final *Freiheit* was not intellectual clarity but was intellectual freedom with its implied moral responsibility is again apparent from the complete absence of evil, here expressed as "Völkerfrieden."

The greatest sin imaginable was skepticism regarding man's perfectibility:

> Nur eine Schmach wirds fürder geben,
> Nur eine Sünde auf der Welt:
> Das ist das eitle Widerstreben,
> Das es für Traum und Wahnsinn hält.
>   (XIV, 34)

The poem "Die Gröszte Sünde" revealed that "das gröszte Laster" was

> ... die nüchterne Schmach, versauert und verteufelt,
> Die an Vervollkommnung der Menschheit stätig zweifelt
> Und die allein die Ursach war bis zu dieser Frist,
> Dasz jener Lebensbaum noch nicht entsprossen ist.
> (XIII, 235)

C. Conclusion

It has been shown that the concepts *Natur* and *Freiheit* were actively present in Keller's thought till 1849 and formed the basis of his optimistic *Weltanschauung*. *Natur* was seen to refer to the tangible forms in nature, but even more to the order of those forms, to the complex of natural laws which in its essence was at rest and closely related to the conception of God, but which in its parts, as individual laws, was purposefully in motion. Man was subject to the laws of nature to the extent that death itself meant a return to nature.

Freiheit referred primarily to intellectual freedom, which was moral freedom based on enlightenment. It was a recognitional freedom which enabled man to understand himself and thus to be himself. It did not imply freedom of action, as man was considered subject to the law of nature. *Freiheit* was the goal of humanity, and its ultimate attainment was assured by the purposeful progress inherent in the passage of time. Keller's early *Weltanschauung* in brief, then, was a deeply religious apprehension of the universe as good and purposeful, and embodied the conviction that man's destiny was to strive through enlightenment and moral freedom to re-enter the purposeful harmony of nature.

CHAPTER II

THE BASIC CONCEPTS *NATUR* AND *FREIHEIT*
1849-1886

In 1848 Gottfried Keller went to the University of Heidelberg to study drama. His philosophic curiosity led him to attend a series of private lectures by the atheist-moralist Ludwig Feuerbach and university lectures substantiating Feuerbach by the anthropologist Karl Henle, and it was not long before Keller accepted the philosophic system of the former with enthusiasm. Feuerbach's logic was too strong for any objections Keller could muster and he had to yield: "Ich liesz mir Schritt für Schritt das Terrain abgewinnen."[1]

Though Keller's disciple-zeal cooled with the years, there existed from this time on a close relationship between many of Keller's philosophic ideas and those of Feuerbach, to the extent that Keller even introduced the latter's logic and terminology in his autobiographical novel, *Der Grüne Heinrich*.[2] Nor can it be disputed that Feuerbach was partially responsible for a number of important changes in Keller's writing at this time: his shift from lyric poetry to prose, his attempted sacrifice of atmosphere and of lyric words to gain an objective style, and his decreased evaluation of emotional experience.

The problem, however, which has not been dealt with successfully to this day is: To what degree did Feuerbach alter Keller's *Weltanschauung*? The complete "Umwälzung" suggested by Dünnebier[3] is not confirmed by the most recent of important Keller critics, Jonas Fränkel.[4] Thus, the question still remains:

---

[1] *Ermatinger* II, 185. Letter to W. Baumgartner, 1849.

[2] A detailed analysis of the parallel ideologies of the two men is to be found in the study by Hans Dünnebier: *Gottfried Keller und Ludwig Feuerbach*.

[3] Hans Dünnebier (*op. cit.*, p. 49), "Diese Weltanschauung, wie sie bisher ihre charakteristischen Seiten hervorgekehrt hat, vom Jüngling begründet, vom Manne geprüft und aufs neue beschworen, sollte binnen einem Vierteljahr einer vollständigen Umwälzung unterliegen, bewirkt durch denselben Philosophen, über den Keller jetzt, Ende des Jahres 1848, den Stab brach, durch Ludwig Feuerbach." To be sure, Dünnebier qualified his statement in other places: "Dieser rasche und durchgreifende Umschwung in Kellers Grundanschauungen innerhalb weniger Monate ist nur möglich beim Zusammentritt innerer Bereitschaft mit eindrucksvollen äuszeren Umständen, indem letzere unbewuszt gehegte Ueberzeugungen erst ins lebendige Bewusztein drängten" (p. 57). "Wie Spinoza für Goethe ... so mag Keller in Feuerbachs Philosophie den rechten Schlüssel für vieles bisher nur dunkel Begriffene gefunden haben" (p. 58).

[4] Jonas Fränkel expressed the opinion that Keller's mature attitude was already set in 1848 before he left for Heidelberg (I, xx). Cf. pp. 106-108 in this study.

Did Feuerbach radically change or merely clarify Keller's attitude? Or, differently stated, were not many of Keller's ideas prior to 1849 essentially in harmony with the philosophy of Feuerbach? Was Keller's *Weltanschauung* in and after 1849 not a consistent outgrowth and continuation of his basic views before 1849?

To begin with, it is significant that Keller was first attracted to Feuerbach because the latter like himself held nature in such high esteem:

> Ich habe aber noch keinen Menschen gesehen, der so frei ist von allem Schulstaub, von allem Schriftdünkel, wie dieser Feuerbach. Er hat nichts als die Natur und wieder die Natur, er ergreift sie mit allen seinen Fibern in ihrer ganzen Tiefe und läszt sich weder von Gott noch Teufel aus ihr herausreiszen.
> (*Ermatinger* II, 185, Letter to W. Baumgartner, Jan., 1849)

Keller suspended decision on Feuerbach until he was convinced that he would not have to alter his own conception of nature very greatly. The question which had worried him the most had been, "wird die Welt, wird das Leben prosaischer und gemeiner nach Feuerbach?" Only when he realized that through Feuerbach nature was to become "klarer und strenger, aber auch glühender und sinnlicher," i.e., a clarification and strengthened reaffirmation of his own previous conception of nature, was Keller willing to accept Feuerbach's thesis.[5]

Keller's statement that he would return to Zürich "in gewissen Dingen verändert" has often been taken to imply a change in basic attitude. A passage from the same letter which included the quotation just mentioned indicates rather a clarification of earlier ideas:

> Wenn es nicht töricht wäre, seinen geistigen Entwicklungsgang bereuen und nicht begreifen zu wollen, so würde ich tief beklagen, dasz ich nicht schon vor Jahren auf ein geregelteres Denken und *gröszere geistige Tätigkeit geführt und so vor vielem gedankenlosem Geschwätz bewahrt worden bin.* (*Ermatinger* II, 182) (my italics)

Keller, here does not bemoan his wrong ideas and misconceptions, but rather the lack of systematic thought with which to assert his ideas. In another passage he shows that Feuerbach did not give him new ideas, but freed him from the confusion and

---

[5] *Ermatinger* II, 185.

THE BASIC CONCEPTS, 1849-1886

lack of conviction which the earlier absence of logic had occasioned:

> Erst jetzt fange ich an, Natur und Mensch so recht zu packen und zu fühlen, und wenn Feuerbach nichts weiter getan hätte, *als dasz er uns von der Unpoesie der spekulativen Theologie und Philosophie erlöste, so wäre das schon ungeheuer viel.* (*Ermatinger* II, 182) (my italics)

Clearly, the ideas with which to grasp "Natur und Mensch" had been present in Keller's mind, but the conviction had been lacking with which to assert himself against speculative theology and philosophy.

These remarks by Keller take on added significance when they are viewed in their historical context. The years which Keller regretted because he had been left exposed to so much "gedankenlosem Geschwätz" can only have been the 1840's,[6] and his comments directed against only one literary group; that of Follen and his associates. Follen, it will be remembered, believed in the unrestrained freedom of the ego and got Keller to introduce this idealism into a number of poems; as when Keller changed the line "tu was du nicht kannst lassen," to "tu was du nicht willst lassen." It is more than understandable that Follen's powerful personality and material security must have made the young poet think twice before rejecting the ideas of such a man in favor of his own. As soon as he acquired a philosophic system to back up his convictions, however, Keller's uncertainty disappeared and he looked back with bitterness on the years of indecision in which he had been unable to refute the arguments of the Follen group and to assert without hesitation his own ideas.

These comments have served to indicate that Keller's outlook after 1849 was primarily a clarification of his earlier attitude. To deal directly with the question of how much his views actually changed, it is now necessary to consider the concepts *Natur* and *Freiheit* as used in his writings in and after 1849.

Prior to 1849 it will be recalled that *Natur* had possessed tangible form and a divinely inspired order. Now, in 1849, one change was apparent; *Natur* no longer reflected the guiding hand of a

---
[6] Keller did not associate with intellectuals in Switzerland until he began to take an active interest in political developments (1843).

personal God. This "atheism" implied little change in Keller's attitude, however, as the following passage reveals:

> Wie es mir bei letzterem (Feuerbach) gehen wird, wage ich noch nicht bestimmt auszusprechen oder zu vermuten . . . Mein Gott war längst nur eine Art von Präsident, oder erster Konsul, welcher nicht viel Ansehen genosz: ich muszte ihn absetzen. Allein ich kann nicht schwören, dasz meine Welt sich nicht wieder an einem schönen Morgen ein Reichsoberhaupt wähle. (*Ermatinger* II, 184, 1849)

Keller could depose or reinstate a personal God with such ease, since the true object of his piety, the purposefulness in nature, was little affected either way. It was in this magnificent purposefulness that he had seen the hand of God active. And not for a second did his faith in that purposefulness waver. The succinct rebuke which the artist, Römer, delivered to the youthful Heinrich was a basic motif of Keller's *Weltanschauungs*-novel: "Die Natur ist vernünftig und zuverlässig."[7] Thus, the elimination of a personal God did not alter materially Keller's attitude toward nature. For a personal God he merely substituted an impersonal reason. As a result, Keller's emotional experience in nature, his piety and love for nature, were little affected:

> Wie trivial erscheint mir gegenwärtig die Meinung, dasz mit dem Aufgeben der sogenannten religiösen Ideen alle Poesie und erhöhte Stimmung aus der Welt verschwinde! Im Gegenteil! Die Welt ist mir unendlich schöner und tiefer geworden . . . (*Ermatinger* II, 275)

In all of Keller's works after 1849 there is the same continued love for nature. In *Die Miszbrauchten Liebesbriefe*, for example, the hero Wilhelm learned, "wie das grüne Erdreich Trost und Kurzweil hat für den Verlassenen." Wilhelm himself loved nature and respected its creatures:

> Denn der Wald war jetzt seine Schulstube . . . Er belauschte das Treiben der Vögel und der andern Tiere, und nie kehrte er zurück, ohne Gaben der Natur in seinem Reisigbündel wohlverwahrt heimzutragen, sei es eine schöne Moosart, ein kunstreiches verlassenes Vogelnest, ein wunderlicher Stein . . . Nur nichts lebendiges heimste er hinein. Je schöner und seltener ein Schmetterling war, den er flattern sah, und es gab auf diesen Höhen deren mehrere Arten, desto andächtiger liesz er ihn fliegen. Denn, sagte er, weisz ich ob der arme Kerl sich schon vermählt hat? Und wenn das nicht

---

[7] XVIII, 27.

wäre, wie abscheulich, die Stammtafel eines so schönen unschuldigen Tieres, welches eine Zierde des Landes ist und eine Freude den Augen mit einem Zuge auszulöschen. (VIII, 184) (my italics)

Dietegen, the hero of the *Novelle* by that name, also loved the sunny fields, the forest, and the animals in nature. The peasants in *Romeo und Julia auf dem Dorfe* were indirectly praised for their appreciation of nature:

> Und da sie dies (taking walks in the woods and finding scenic spots and views) offenbar nicht zu ihrer Pönitenz tun, sondern zu ihrem Vergnügen, so ist wohl anzunehmen, dasz sie Sinn für die Natur haben, auch abgesehen von ihrer Nützlichkeit. (VII, 161)

Keller's continued deep regard for nature expressed itself on almost every page of his works in his constant use of the adjective "natürlich," and its associates "unverdorben," "gesund," "ursprünglich," "rein," unbefangen," "einfach," to designate a person or thing worthy of his favor. His use of these adjectives is so profuse that examples may be picked at random:

> Indem es ihm unvermutet einfiel, dasz dergleichen *unbefangene* Scherze, frohes Benehmen und Zutraulichkeit, ja eben die Kennzeichen und Sitten feiner, *natürlicher*, und wohlgearteter Menschen und einer glücklichen Geselligkeit wären ... (XIX, 243, *Der Grüne Heinrich* IV) (my italics)

> Der *natürliche* Mensch betrachtet sich selbst als einen Teil vom Ganzen und darum ebenso *unbefangen* wie dieses ... (XVII, 201, *Der Grüne Heinrich* II) (my italics)

> Es ist die königliche Gesinnung eines *ursprünglichen* und *reinen* Menschen, welche, allgemein verbreitet, die Gesellschaft in eine Republik von lauter liebevollen und wahrhaft adelig gesinnten Königen verwandeln würde: (XVI, 27, *Der Grüne Heinrich* I) (my italics)

> Da ich zugleich die Städte vermied und meinen Arbeitsverkehr immer im freien Felde, auf Bergen und in Wäldern betrieb, wo nur *ursprüngliche* und *einfache* Menschen waren, so reiste ich wirklich wie zu der Zeit der Patriarchen. (VII, 30 *Pankraz der Schmoller*) (my italics)

> Er wies mich an, hohle, zerrissene Weidenstrünke, verwitterte Bäume und abenteuerliche Felsgespenster aufzusuchen mit den bunten Farben der Fäulnis und des Zerfalles ... Doch die Natur bot sie mir nur spärlich, sich einer volleren *Gesundheit* erfreuend als mit meinen Wünschen verträglich war. (XVII, 122, *Der Grüne Heinrich* II) (my italics—typical significance of *gesund* though not in adjective form)

Though the loss of a personal God did not affect Keller's conception of nature greatly, there is still a possibility that other less obvious influences such as his anatomy studies or his futile love for Johanna Kapp[8] might have done so, and the only way to discount these is to demonstrate that *Natur* remained unchanged in all of its various aspects.

It can be shown that *Natur* retained her outer form. Many quotations might be cited to substantiate the following passage from *Der Grüne Heinrich*:

> Die Mehrheit ... ist die einzige, wirkliche und notwendige Macht im Lande, *so greifbar und fühlbar wie die körperliche Natur selbst*, an die wir gefesselt sind. (XIX, 317) (my italics)

Secondly, *Natur* still possessed her internal order, which is not surprising in view of the fact that Keller did not surrender his faith in nature's purposefulness. Frequent references to natural law are made in *Der Grüne Heinrich*, a few of which may be given here:

> In der Tat ist aber beides gleich leicht und gleich schwer zu lernen, das Wesentliche wie das Unwesentliche, wenn es nur zur rechten Stunde geschieht, und die Verkennung dieser Tatsache, welche mit dem *Gesetz der Natur* innig verbunden ist, ... (XIX, 44) (my italics)

> So fest und allgemein wie *das Naturgesetz* selber sollen wir unser Dasein durch das nähren, was wir sind und bedeuten. (XIX, 82) (my italics)

> Das Glück des Wissens ... weiset vorwärts und nicht zurück und läszt über *den unabänderlichen Bestand und Leben des Gesetzes* die eigene Vergänglichkeit vergessen. (XIX, 33) (my italics)

> Das harte Wort: "Ein Geschlecht vergeht und das andere entsteht!" verlor die scheinbare Kälte seiner *Notwendigkeit*. (XVII, 91) (my italics)

If one skims over the entire period to his last work, *Martin Salander*, the same belief in natural law is still evident:

> Ueber Naturgesetze hat die Republik nicht zu bestimmen. (*Hertz* VIII, 92)

> Es ist ein Naturgesetz, dasz alles Leben, je rastloser es gelebt werde, um so schneller sich auslebe und ein Ende nähme ... (*Hertz* VIII, 160)

---

[8] Hochdorf thought for a time that Johanna Kapp had caused Keller's change of attitude in 1849 (*Gottfried Keller im europäischen Gedanken*, p. 27).

Thirdly, *Ruhe* continued to be the essence of nature.[9] Occasionally Keller made a specific statement to this effect such as in the description of the nature paintings of Salomon Landolt, whom Keller wanted to show as an enlightened person:

> Der unablässige Wandel, das Aufglimmen und verklingen der *innerlich ruhigen Natur* schienen nur die wechselnden Akkorde desselben Tonstückes zu sein. (*Hertz* VI, 211) (my italics)

But Keller more often made use of *Ruhe* to describe the state of mind of an enlightened person who had come to identify himself with nature; an enlightened person regained the *Ruhe* which was the essence of nature and of himself as a part of nature.[10] In the light of Keller's new clear-cut belief in human mortality,[11] "Abendlied" (1887) shows that death meant a return to rest in nature:

> Fallen einst die müden Lider zu,
> Löscht ihr aus, *dann hat die Seele Ruh*;
> Tastend streift sie ab die Wanderschuh,
> Legt sich auch in ihre finstre Truh.
> (my italics) (I, 40)

In 1880 Keller indicated in a letter written to his friend Wilhelm Petersen that death was identical with *Ruhe*:

> Es hat etwas Unbequemes, in diesen Jahren so herumwandern zu müssen; allein das Ganze ist ja doch nur ein Bummel und am Ende kommt die Ruhe. (*Ermatinger* III, 320)

Salomon Landolt conceived death to be "wechsellose Ruhe."[12] In its essential features, then, *Natur* remained the same after 1849 as before. Keller had interpreted Feuerbach's statement "Gott ist Natur" in such a way that his basic piety and faith remained unchanged.

At this point a word is in place regarding Keller's new belief in mortality. This conviction was expressed very clearly in a poem of 1849:

> Ich hab in kalten Wintertagen,
> In dunkler, hoffnungsarmer Zeit
> Ganz aus dem Sinne dich geschlagen,
> O Trugbild der Unsterblichkeit!

---

[9] This thesis is supported by Hans Dünnebier, though in the belief that it revealed a drastic change in Keller's attitude (*op. cit.*, pp. 74-75): "Jetzt dagegen heiszt es: Gott ist die Ruhe."
[10] Cf. pp. 64-65 in this study.
[11] *Ermatinger* II, 275.
[12] *Hertz* VI, 153.

> Nun, da der Sommer glüht und glänzet,
> Nun seh' ich, dasz ich wohlgetan;
> Ich habe neu das Herz umkränzet,
> Im Grabe aber liegt der Wahn.
>
> ― ― ―
>
> Nun erst versteh' ich, die da blühet,
> O Lilie, deinen stillen Grusz,
> Ich weisz, wie hell die Flamme glühet,
> Dasz ich gleich dir vergehen musz!
> (I, 213, *Gesammelte Gedichte*)

Human mortality remained a recurrent theme: In *Romeo und Julia auf dem Dorfe* (1856) after the lovers tired of kissing, the awareness of death intruded itself:

> Sie umhalsten sich und küszten sich unverweilt und so lange, bis sie einstweilen müde waren, oder wie man es nennen will, wenn das Küssen zweier Verliebter auf eine oder zwei Minuten sich selbst überlebt und die Vergänglichkeit alles Lebens mitten im Rausche der Blütezeit ahnen läszt. (VII, 135)

In *Kleider machen Leute* (ca. 1860) the romantic tailor meditated "wie vergänglich alles Glück sei" (VIII, 25). In the "Becherlied" (1862) are lines which indicate the mortality of all things:

> Wie Glück und Glas so leicht zerbricht,
> Nur etwas später bricht das Erz. (I, 255)

Keller's belief in mortality came in later years to be expressed almost consistently in the one succinct phrase: "Alles nimmt ein Ende." Thus in the *Narr von Manegg* (1877) was the passage:

> Dieser Manesse starb hochbetagt, wenn ich nicht irre, um das Jahr 1380; mit ihm sank aber der Stern jener Linie; seine Söhne lebten sternlos dahin, wie alles ein Ende nimmt . . . (*Hertz* VI, 125)

In the *Landvogt von Greifensee* Aglaja commented after a happy few hours spent with Landolt: "So nimmt alles ein Ende" (*Hertz* VI, 159). In the first few pages of *Martin Salander* (1866) appeared the words, "wie alles hienieden allmählich sein Ende erreicht." Toward the end of the novel came the telltale phrase:

> Wie aber alles Menschliche *ein Ende nimmt*, ging es auch hier dem Feierabend so vielen Unrechtes und Leidens entgegen. (*Hertz* VIII, 196) (my italics)

Without doubt Feuerbach was the cause for this new conviction. But there is no reason, as Dünnebier maintains,[13] to believe that the idea of mortality was something radically new in Keller's thought. Both "Wetternacht" and "Der alte Bettler" had chanted the same refrain as "Abendlied," that death was a return to rest in nature; as early as 1845, immortality had resembled an impersonalized sleep in nature. Here again Feuerbach's influence had brought about a clarification of attitude rather than an actual change. For that matter, as a case in simple psychology, the enthusiasm with which Keller greeted the thesis of mortality was in itself evidence that he had found corroboration for his own ideas. Feuerbach must be given his due. By clarifying Keller's views on mortality and removing his last hopes of a personal God, he had indeed ended the latter's lyric period and brought him to maturity. His contribution however had not been to give Keller new ideas, but to provide him with a systematic, philosophic basis for his convictions.

What, now, happened during the Heidelberg period to *Freiheit*? On the strength of Keller's "new belief in mortality," Dünnebier had asserted: "Die Subjektivität wird überwunden, der schrankenlose Geist der Freiheit in engere Schranken eingedämmt."[14] Though it has been shown that *Freiheit* even before 1849 was not "unlimited" (*schrankenlos*) it will be well to reexamine the concept as it appeared after 1849; and since Keller's mature philosophy of freewill was treated most specifically in *Der Grüne Heinrich*, the following discussion is based primarily upon this novel. The subsequent works of the period will be treated in chronological fashion further along.

Although he denied the existence of a God, Feuerbach had not taught an out-and-out materialism. He had retained the concept of an immaterial soul:

> *Materialismus* ist eine durchaus unpassende, falsche Vorstellungen mit sich führende Bezeichnung, nur insofern zu entschuldigen, als der Immaterialität des Denkens, der Seele, die Materialität des Denkens entgegensteht.[15]

Feuerbach had been able to retain an immaterial reality in his doctrine through the concept of the organism:

---

[13] *Op. cit.*, 79-80.
[14] *Op. cit.*, 73.
[15] Quoted by Hans Dünnebier, *op. cit.*, 176. The passage was one of Feuerbach's *Nachgelassene Aphorismen*.

> Aber es gibt für uns nur ein organisches Leben. Also Organismus ist der rechte Ausdruck, denn der Spiritualist leugnet, dasz das Denken eines Organs bedürfe, während auf dem Standpunkt der Naturforschung es keine Tätigkeit ohne Organe gibt.[16]

Keller took over the concept of the organism. Its importance was stressed early in *Der Grüne Heinrich* when the youth was being instructed in botany:

> Nachdem er uns die äuszerliche Stellung der Pflanzen in der Natur klar gemacht und uns für sie eingenommen hatte, ging er auf ihre allgemeinen Eigenschaften und auf die Erklärung ihres Organismus über, wobei wir die ersten Blicke in die Bedeutung dieses Wortes erhielten, welches wir von nun an nicht vergaszen. (XVI, 251)

An organism was for Keller more than the sum of its parts, just as products such as a cradle, a table, and a coffin were more than the sum of their parts.[17] These structures were not merely the pine slabs used in their construction. Nor was a rose merely a conglomeration of potash and other elements:

> Ihre Zeit hat auch die Rose. Wer wird, wenn sie erblüht um sie herumspringen und rufen: He! das ist nichts als Pottasche und einige andere Stoffe ... (XIX, 48)

To cap his argument that materials and product are not coincidental, Keller remarked that while the idealist Schiller had stimulated himself in the writing of his dramas with the odor of rotting apples, which almost caused the realist Goethe to faint, the odor of the apples is nowhere apparent in his idealistic dramas.[17]

Keller then applied his thesis, that materials and finished product differed and that the whole was more than the sum of its parts, to his discussion of freewill. The anthropology professor, he concluded, had been unable to distinguish between "des hervorbringenden lebendigen Ackergrundes ... zu gunsten des Hervorgebrachten, der moralischen Frucht, als ob eine Aehre und eine Erdscholle nicht unzweifelhaft zwei Dinge, zwei Gegenstände sei." For Keller the human organism was also a product, also differed from the sum of its parts, and could quite logically still *possess a freewill*:

> Es reizte Heinrich ... seinen moralischen freien Willen als in dessen Gesamtorganismus begründet, und als dessen höchstes Gut, aufzufinden. (XIX, 49)

---

[16] *Ibid.*
[17] XIX, 47.

There was in the organism at the outset an idea, a purpose, a moral kernel from which the freewill developed:

> Vielmehr geriet er auf den natürlichen[18] Gedanken, dasz das Wahrste und beste hier wohl in der Mitte liegen dürfte, dasz innerhalb des ununterbrochenen organischen Verhaltens, der darin eingeschachtelten Reihenfolge der Eindrücke, Erfahrungen, Vorstellungen, *zuinnerst der moralische Fruchtkern eines freien Willens keime zum emporstrebenden Baume*, dessen Aeste gleichwohl wieder sich zum Grunde hinabbögen, dem sie entsprossen, um dort unauflässig aufs neue Wurzeln zu schlagen. (XIX, 50-51) (my italics)

The moral kernel, the essence of the organism, germinated into a freewill which, however, retained its contact with the physical reality wherein it was conceived. This moral kernel Keller then showed in a symbolical description of a riding gallery to be the moral law. The gallery was the material substance of the world. The horse was the "immer noch materielle Organ." The rider was "der gute menschliche Wille, welches jenes zu beherrschen und zum freien Willen zu werden trachtet." And the riding master was "das moralische Gesetz, das aber einzig und allein auf die Natur und Eigenschaften des Pferdes gegründet ist, und ohne dieses gar nicht vorhanden wäre" (XIX, 51).

The moral law was *the natural law of mankind*. Keller did not state this fact in so many words, but four aspects of the moral law indicate that it was a part of the harmony of natural laws which applied, however, solely to man.

Firstly, the moral law was not purely a spiritual or abstract force, but, as has just been indicated, was completely dependent on the organism and its particular characteristics. Furthermore it expressed itself as a physical urge. The designation commonly used by Keller for this urge was "innere Notwendigkeit" with its synonyms "reiner Trieb," "innerer Antrieb," "innewohnende Kraft," "Innerlichkeit," "lebendige Innerlichkeit." Just like other natural laws, then, the moral law expressed itself in physical terms.

Secondly, the moral law possessed the merciless regularity and impartiality of natural law:

> Wie er nun dazu noch sah, dasz jede geschichtliche Erscheinung genau die Dauer hat, welche ihre Gründlichkeit und lebendige Innerlichkeit verdient und der Art ihres Entstehens entspricht, wie die Dauer jedes Erfolges nur die Abrechnung der verwendeten Mittel und die Prüfung des Verständnisses ist und wie gegen

---

[18] "Natürlich" reveals Keller's agreement with the idea.

> die ununterbrochene Ursachenreihe auch in der Geschichte weder
> hoffen noch fürchten, weder jammern noch toben, weder Uebermut
> noch Verzagtheit etwas hilft, sondern Bewegung und Rückschlag
> ihren wohlgemessenen und begründeten Rhythmus haben . . . Dies
> alles betrieb er . . . lediglich um die eine moralische Anschauung
> von allen Dingen zu verstärken. (XIX, 68)

Thirdly, moral law had the dynamic purposefulness of natural law. Keller felt that the progressive development in the history of mankind was the tangible result of the moral law at work. The study of the history of Roman law had shown "wie das ganze Wesen, dem Rechts- und Freiheitsgefühl einer Rasse entsprossen" (XIX, 58). The study of the earliest human institutions had offered evidence that they too had developed out of this "Rechtsgefühl":

> Die uralte heilige Ehrbarkeit, mit welcher in der Menschensprache
> überall das Abgeteilte, Zahl, Masz und Gewicht, Trockenes und
> Flüssiges, Bodeneinteilung und Geschlechtsverwandschaft erschienen, wies von selbst wieder hin auf die Rechtsgeschichte und bestätigte deren Qualität in der Menschennatur. (XIX, 59)

Moral law made history from an arbitrary sequence of human events into an "organisch-notwendiges Gewebe" (XIX, 60), in which there was only a progress upwards. The moral law was the law of history. There was no law of retrogression, "d.h. der Rückschritt ist nichts anderes als der stockende Fortschritt" (XIX, 61).

Fourthly, the moral law had the universality of natural law. This fact is already implicit in the quotations just given, but it is even more apparent in a passage which referred to Heinrich when he had almost reached the peak of his development:

> Er studierte jetzt verschiedene Geschichtsvorgänge ganz im einzelnen in ihrer faktischen und rhetorischen Dialektik, und fast war
> es ihm gleichgültig, was für ein Vorgang es war, überall nur das
> Eine und Alles sehend, was in allen Dingen wirkt und treibt, und
> eben dieses Eine packen lernend, wie junge Füchse eine Wachtel.
> (XIX, 253)

Thus, the moral law was the natural law of humanity. It was the one motivating force in all of man's doings. At the same time it was also the kernel of freewill, the riding master that led the human will to freewill. Being both an immutable law of nature and the drive to freewill, the moral law guaranteed man eventual freedom.

What now was this "predetermined" freewill of man? It was a quality which mankind acquired gradually:

> Sogleich sagte ihm ein guter Sinn, dasz wenn auch dieser freie Wille ursprünglich in den ersten Geschlechtern und auch jetzt noch in wilden Völkerstämmen und verwahrlosten Einzelnen nicht vorhanden, derselbe sich doch einfinden und *auswachsen muszte*, sobald die Frage nach ihm sich einfand. (XIX, 49) (my italics)

Freewill was based on enlightenment:

> Während Heinrich ohne freien Willen, denn er konnte gar nicht anders, rücksichtslos und gänzlich die Zeit verwendete, sich Zeug und Stoff für seinen freien Willen zu verschaffen, nämlich *Einsicht* ... (XIX, 69) (my italics) [19]

Absolute enlightenment, which implies freewill, brought happiness to mankind and an end to evil:

> Es handelt sich aber eben in der Geschichte und Politik um das, was die kurzsichtigen Helden und Rhetoren nie einsehen; nicht um ein Trauerspiel, sondern um ein gutes Ziel und Ende, wo *die geläuterte, unbedingte Einsicht* alle versöhnt, um ein groszes heiteres Lustspiel, wo niemand mehr blutet und niemand mehr weint. Langsam aber sicher geht die Welt diesem Ziele entgegen. (XIX, 66) (my italics)

Freewill thus implied moral conduct based on enlightenment and was very similar in its essential features to the ideal of intellectual freedom held by Keller before 1849. The only new feature was that Keller placed the driving force not in the divinely inspired law of time, but within man himself as his own personal law.[20]

A person who had acquired freewill was characterized in Keller's eyes by "eine feste ruhige Gleichmut" since such an atti-

---

[19] Note that here, in the original version, it is the author who is speaking.

[20] Time became a relative concept as it existed in "verschiedene Zeiträume": "Welch ein Ersatz für das hergebrachte begriffslose Wort Ewigkeit ist die Kenntnisnahme von der Entfernung der Himmelskörper und der Schnelligkeit des Lichtes, von der Tatsache, dasz wir allaugenblicklich Licht, also Körper mit ihren Schicksalen, in ihrem Bestehen, wahrnehmen, welches vor einem Jahre, vor hundert, tausend und mehr Jahren gewesen ist, dasz wir also mit einem Blick tausend Existenzen tausend verschiedener Zeiträume auffassen, vom nächsten Baume an, welchen wir gleichzeitig mit seinem wirklichen augenblicklichen Dasein wahrnehmen, bis zu dem fernsten Stern, dessen Licht länger unterwegs ist als das Menschengeschlecht unseres Wissens besteht ... Wo bleibt da noch eine Unruhe, ein zweifelhaftes Sehnen nach einer unbegriffenen Ewigkeit, wenn wir sehen, dasz alles entsteht und vergeht, sein Dasein abmiszt nacheinander und doch wieder zumal ist" (XIX, 36)? Cf. also XIX, 165, with its discussion of the relativity of time in a dream and the realization that an entire dream can be lived in a second. Cf. also, the poem "Die Zeit geht nicht" (I, 214). The relativity of time did not alter Keller's faith in a future Utopia as may be noted from the quotations.

tude developed from an awareness of the purposefulness in history (i.e., of the moral law):

> Der ruhige feste Gleichmut, welcher aus solcher Auffassung des Ganzen und Vergleichung des Einzelnen hervorgeht . . . macht erst den guten und wohlgebildeten Weltbürger aus. (XIX, 60)

Ruhig sein did not imply intellectual resignation or a restriction of the fields of intellectual query.[21] The enlightened count in *Der Grüne Heinrich*, whose very grasp, glance, and voice revealed that he was "der freie Mensch, der über den zufälligen Dingen steht," made clear that *ruhig bleiben* meant not a restriction of the intellect but rather the calm which revealed an enlightened and open mind:

> Es handelt sich um das Recht, ruhig zu bleiben im Gemüt, *was auch die Ergebnisse des Nachdenkens und des Forschens* sein mögen, und unangetastet und ungekränkt zu bleiben, was man auch mit wahrem und ehrlichem Sinne glauben mag. *Uebrigens geht der Mensch in die Schule alle Tage* und keiner vermag mit Sicherheit vorauszusagen was er am Abend seines Lebens glauben werde; Dafür haben wir die unbedingte *Freiheit des Gewissens nach allen Seiten!* (XIX, 264) (my italics)

Almost two decades later in *Das Verlorene Lachen* (1874) Keller restated his position and showed again that the quiet which came with intellectual freedom was not an indication of resignation:

> Aber die gewonnene Stille und Ruhe ist nicht der Tod, sondern das Leben, das fortblüht und leuchtet, wie dieser Sonntagsmorgen, und guten Gewissens wandeln wir hindurch, der Dinge gewärtig, die kommen oder nicht kommen werden. (VIII, 429)

The correlation of *Ruhe* with intellectual freedom in an enlightened individual has an especial significance since Keller's artistic principles led him henceforth to employ in his writing symbolical pictures rather than categorical terms.[22] Thus, instead of speaking of a person as having freewill, he revealed the fact to a sharp-eyed observer by showing in the course of the action that the person was inwardly *ruhig*. An excellent illustration of this stylistic procedure is found in the *Novelle*, *Frau*

---

[21] For Ermatinger's position, cf. app., pp. 172-173.

[22] For a discussion of Keller's symbolism, cf. pp. 113-114 in this study. Keller also avoided key-words because he felt that "wer die Worte Natur, Biederkeit, Gefühl, Herz, usw. immer im Munde führt, ist gewöhnlich ein verzwickter Geselle." (*Ermatinger* II, 355, letter of 1854.)

Regel Amrain und ihr Jüngster, where the hero is first educated to an enlightened, free outlook and then is shown in a critical situation to possess the tell-tale, inner *Ruhe*.

Frau Regula guided her son toward an enlightened attitude in a number of ways. She was careful never to impede the youth's "freie Bewegungen."[23] She accustomed him to thrift and personal independence by allowing "ihm eine kleine Sparbüchse zu gänzlich freier Verfügung."[24] She never allowed him for a moment to be what he was not and thus to impair a correct understanding of inner necessity:

> Wenn er dagegen nur die leiseste Neigung verriet, sich irgend Eigenschaften beizulegen, die er nicht besasz, oder etwas zu übertreiben, was ihm gut zu stehen schien, oder sich zu zieren, so tadelte sie ihn mit schneidenden, harten Worten. (VII, 205)

She taught him to be "freisinnig" in the fullest sense of the word, and quickly checked any tendencies to empty talk, slogans, and partisanship (VII, 220). In a word, as Keller ultimately confides to the reader, this ideal pedagogue imbued Fritz with her own "Denkungsart" (VII, 202). Frau Regula made Fritz into a model man, a fact which is brought out symbolically at the end of the story. In answer to his good-for-nothing father's wordy assertion that he intended to invest money in the family business, Fritz showed his maturity and enlightenment by not losing his calm:

> Sein Sohn schenkte ihm aber *ruhig* ein anderes Glas Wein ein und sagte: "Vater, ich wollte Euch raten, dasz Ihr . . . es Euch wohl sein lasset . . . Wenn Ihr . . . ein Engel vom Himmel wäret, so würde ich Euch nicht zum förmlichen Anteilhaber nehmen, weil Ihr das Werk nicht gelernt habt und, verzeiht mir meine Unhöflichkeit, nicht versteht!" Der Alte . . . sah, dasz sein Sohn wuszte, was er wollte. (VII, 254) (my italics)

Thus, Keller shows clearly that Fritz had acquired intellectual freedom, but with a laconic and subtle artistry that demands both alertness and understanding on the part of the reader.

Perhaps the best way to impart Keller's conception of freewill is to show his portrayal of a free individual in comparison with an unfree one. It will be recalled that at the party following the artists' festival in Munich, Ferdinand Lys left his escort in Hein-

---
[23] VII, 202.
[24] *Ibid.*, 203.

rich's care and spent his entire time in the company of the hostess Rosalie. In conventional eyes, Lys displayed a lack of loyalty; and Heinrich, considering the conduct of Lys unethical, took it upon himself to defend the maidenly virtue of the neglected Agnes. In the development Lys was first shown to be an egoist by nature:

> Wegen des Zusammentreffens seines groszen Reichtumes, seiner Einsamkeit und seines genuszdürftigen Witzes ein groszer Egoist. (XVIII, 123)

Nevertheless, he was a profound and sincere person. He had become a realist after a visit to Italy:

> Er wurde ein Realist und gewann von Tag zu Tag eine solche Kraft und Tiefe in der Empfindung des Lebens und des Menschlichen, dasz die Ueberlieferung seiner Jugend und Schülerzeit dagegen erbleichen muszte. (XVIII, 124)

He refused to act against his convictions:

> Alle diese Wiedersprüche zu überwinden und ihnen zum Trotz das darzustellen, was er nicht fühlte noch glaubte, aber es durch die Energie seines Talentes doch zum Leben zu bringen, dazu war er zu sehr Philosoph. (XVIII, 126)

To Heinrich's accusation that he had acted unethically, Lys replied:

> Ich sage noch einmal, du verstehst das nicht! . . . Ich will dich nicht an deine Jugendgeschichte erinnern . . . *Denn du hast getan was du nicht lassen konntest, du tust es jetzt, ud du wirst es tun, so lange du lebst* . . . Du wirst zu jeder Zeit das lassen, was dir nicht angenehm ist. Angenehm oder unangenehm aber ist nicht nur alles Sinnliche, sondern auch die moralischen Hirngespinste sind es. So bist du jetzt sinnlich verliebt in das eigentümliche Mädchen. Dies ist dir angenehm, aber weil du wohl merkst, dasz du dabei kein rechtes Herz hast, nicht in deinem eigentlichen Sinne liebst, so verbindest du mit jenem Reiz noch die moralische Annehmlichkeit, dich für das schmale Wesen ins Zeug zu werfen und den uneigennützigen Beschützer zu machen. Wisse aber, wenn du einen Funken eigentlicher Liebe verspürtest, so würdest und müsztest du allein darnach trachten, deinen Schützling meinem Bereiche zu entziehen. (Dorothea awakened this feeling in Heinrich later on.) Du hast aber die wahre Leidenschaft noch nie gekannt, weder in meinem noch in deinem Sinne. Was du als halbes Kind erlebt, war das blosze Erwachen deines Bewusztseins . . . (XVIII, 238) (my italics)

THE BASIC CONCEPTS, 1849-1886   67

Lys recognized man's adherence to natural law:

> Wisse ferner, was mich betrifft: jeder ganze Mann musz jedes annehmliche Weib sogleich lieben, sei es für kürzer, länger, oder immer, der Unterschied der Dauer liegt blosz in den aüszeren Umständen. Das Auge ist der Urheber, der Vermittler und der Erhalter oder Vernichter der Liebe; ich kann mir vornehmen, treu zu sein, *aber das Auge nimmt sich nichts vor, das gehorcht und fügt sich der ewigen Naturgesetze.* Luther hat nur als Normalmann gesprochen ... wenn er sagte, er könne kein Weib ansehen ohne ihrer zu begehren! (XVIII, 238) (my italics)

Lys had turned to Rosalie because she represented his ideal:

> Erst durch ein Weib, welches durch spezifisches Wesen, durch Reinheit von allem eigensinnigen, kränklichen und absonderlichen Beiwerke eine Darstellung einer ganzen Welt von Weibern ist, durch ein Weib von so unverwüstlicher Gesundheit wie diese Rosalie— kann ein kluger Mann für immer gefesselt werden. (XVIII, 239)

Lys felt his personal freedom, his freewill:

> Ich habe keine Hoffnungen angeregt, *ich bin frei und meines Willens Herr*, gegen ein Weib sowohl wie gegen alle Welt. Uebrigens werde ich für das gute Kind tun was ich kann und ihr ein wahrer und uneigennütziger Freund sein ohne Ziererei und ohne Phrasen. (XVIII, 240, (my italics)

However, Henrich too, felt his personal freedom:

> Ich hoffe, dasz ich immer weniger das tue, was ich lassen kann, und dasz ich zu jeder Zeit etwas lassen kann, das schlecht und verwerflich ist, sobald ich es nur erkenne. (XVIII, 237)

Heinrich berated Lys for lack of "Treue," "Ehre," and "Glauben" until Lys finally felt compelled to challenge Heinrich to a duel. Lys then went home and calmly thought things out. He was reconciled to his fate, felt sorry for Heinrich, and understood both how the incident had arisen and why its tragic climax had been unavoidable. It was his hope that should he die, his death would serve to open Heinrich's eyes. He blushed as he looked at his rather erotic album of former sweethearts and tossed it in the fire.[25]

Heinrich, on the other hand, did not dare to go home. He knew instinctively that as soon as he had recovered from his excitement and fatigue, his inner voice would show him the folly of his act.[26] Thus Heinrich, although he was already overstimulated by wine and lack of sleep, spent the night drinking in a tavern.

---
[25] XVIII, 242.
[26] XVIII, 243.

In this incident as narrated by Keller, it is obvious that Lys was the individual who possessed freewill, for he alone recognized the immutable force of natural law, and condemned all arbitrary, "moralische Hirngespinste." Lys remained faithful to the law of his own organism. He showed calm self-possession, sincerity, and intellectual freedom.

Heinrich had been sincere in his actions, but he did not have sufficient insight to know that the sensation of manly power he experienced was caused by wine and lack of sleep. As a result, he had become "eine Abirrung von sich selbst" because of the disharmony between his inner impulse and his actions. This disregard for his own personal law led to tragedy: he killed his best friend.[27]

Keller's philosophy in action revealed then the same conception of freewill as before: freedom of moral decision based on enlightenment. Freewill implied the ability to recognize that man was subject to immutable natural laws. It implied the ability to recognize that man possessed a personal law, the moral law, which a far-sighted nature had designed to fit him into the harmonious scheme of the universe. It implied obedience to the moral law, based on man's realization that his nature demanded such action if happiness and morality were to exist. Thus the basic freedom for Keller, as expressed in *Der Grüne Heinrich*, was practically identical with the intellectual freedom which he had extolled in his writings prior to 1849.

During the preceding discussion of freewill in *Der Grüne Heinrich*, the reader may well have been saying to himself: "This is all very well. But since Heinrich only matured at the end of the story after he learned from the Count and Dorothea to disavow his belief in God and immortality, how can his university views represent Keller's views in 1850?"

A number of factors indicate that this correlation is permissible. For one thing, the stay at the home of the count and the sojourn at the university were really a concurrent experience for Heinrich and were separated by Keller only for purposes of poetic simplification: to allow presentation of the youth's new ideas on freewill apart from his views on God and immortality, and to allow also a lightening of the heavy philosophical con-

---

[27] Lys died later from the wound inflicted by Heinrich. In the revised version, Lys stops the duel (V, 282).

tent through insertion of narrative material. Feuerbach's teachings were the basis of both experiences. At the university, Heinrich developed his ideas on freewill in terms of Feuerbach's concept of the organism, after learning from anatomy lectures that God was not needed to explain the purposeful structure in man and nature; i.e., he based his defense of freewill on the same atheistic idealism that Feuerbach taught. At the home of the count, who was a Feuerbach enthusiast (some scholars think he was created after Feuerbach himself[28]), Heinrich acquired the notion that even the soul of man was mortal. The concurrent nature of these scenes is also evident from the fact that Keller had thought about both ideas, freewill and mortality, while at Heidelberg.

Heinrich did not change his conception of freewill radically during his stay with the count. It was Heinrich's new belief in mortality, to be sure, that made him feel he had finally acquired "völlige Geistesfreiheit" (XIX, 270), but such freedom certainly did not entail more than enlightenment and moral discernment and so differed little from the concept of freewill he had formulated at the university. There, already, he had decided that "Einsicht" led to freewill, and that only "unbedingte geläuterte Einsicht" would eliminate tragedy from the world. Universal insight of this nature is synonymous with intellectual freedom and equivalent to "völlige Geistesfreiheit."

Thus, because Feuerbach was the inspiration of Heinrich's thought both at the university and at the home of the Count, and because Heinrich's concept of freewill did not change perceptibly even though he himself had acquired greater insight, Heinrich's university views have been taken as representing Keller's conception of freewill in the 1850's.

But again the reader may object: "If then, the views of the mature Heinrich be allowed to stand, why should not those of the youthful Heinrich represent the views of the young Keller?" Though there is obviously much autobiographical material in the story and character of the youthful Heinrich, there are nevertheless good reasons for not taking all his views, especially his views on *Freiheit,* as coincidental with those of the young Keller. *Der Grüne Heinrich* was written in the half-decade following Keller's Heidelberg stay, when he was still living in the

---

[28] Cf. For example, Dünnebier, *op. cit.,* p. 142.

emotional and intellectual world which had inspired him to write the book; figuratively speaking, he was still the mature Heinrich, and thus had no difficulty in being true to his Heidelberg views. His youthful outlook, on the other hand, he could only relive in the light of his later views. Dünnebier substantiates this point:

> Es sei hier nochmals betont, dasz der grüne Heinrich nicht in allen Stücken der junge Gottfried Keller ist. In der Jugendgeschichte sind Dinge und Geschehnisse von einem Standpunkt aus gesehen und beurteilt, den der Dichter erst später gewonnen hat. (*op. cit.*, p. 68)

Secondly, Keller wrote the novel to show the development of a youthful personality from subjectivity to objectivity, from spiritualism to enlightened materialism, from romanticism to realism. He wanted to share with the world his enlightened views. It was not difficult to let the mature Heinrich be an accurate picture of himself and his attitude. The mixed views of his youth, however, were far too complex and contradictory to be easily presented and had to be simplified to pure romanticism for purposes of poetic clarity. His own complex development would not have permitted the "Uebersichtlichkeit" he always strove to achieve.[29] Thirdly, facts already presented have shown that Keller's early views on *Freiheit* and *Natur,* enlightenment and the natural order, were not typically romantic. To be sure, *Natur* possessed definite romantic elements, but, as Käthe Heesch agrees,[30] nature was by no means thoroughly romantic. Good enough reasons, all, it would then seem, for avoiding too general an identification of young Heinrich with the young Keller.

It will now be shown that this conception of freewill based on enlightenment remained with Keller throughout the rest of his literary life as a fundamental part of his attitude. *Der Grüne Heinrich*, which formed the basis of the preceding discussion, reflected Keller's attitude during the years of its writing, 1849-1855. To offset any argument that Keller had changed his mind toward the end of the work, and had different opinions on freedom when he wrote book four from those he held when he wrote book one, a letter of 1851 from Keller to his friend Wilhelm Baumgartner may be mentioned, in which Keller had stressed,

---

[29] Cf. pp. 111-114 in this study.
[30] Cf. app., p. 154.

"nach und nach werden alle Menschen zur klaren Erkenntnis kommen."[31]

Keller's attitude during the years 1855-1859 is mirrored in the *Sinngedicht*, which was conceived in these years, although not put into written form until 1881. The *Sinngedicht*, an apotheosis of intellectual freedom in Keller's sense, is the most complex and perhaps the most profound of Keller's works. It has three motifs which are developed simultaneously. At first sight, the *Sinngedicht* reveals a charming love story. A closer consideration shows that it is the expression of Keller's views on marriage and the nature of the sexes. A philosophical analysis brings to light a profound symbolism which reflected Keller's basic views on determinism and idealism. As Keller abhorred allegory above all else, the three themes play into one another, and flesh-and-blood reality is never forsaken for abstract values.

The hero of the *Sinngedicht*, Reinhart, was a physicist. Symbolically, he typified an aggressive male with the views of a man on marriage and the relation of the sexes; allegorically he represented a belief in the sole validity of scientific, natural law. To be sure, he had learned of the existence of the moral law in his youth:

> ... um von der Gesetzmäszigkeit und dem Zusammenhang der moralischen Welt überzeugt zu werden und wie überall nicht ein Wort fällt, welches nicht Ursache und Wirkung zugleich wäre, wenn auch so gering wie das Säuseln des Grashalmes auf einer Wiese. (XI, 3)

But as a scientist, he had come to restrict his attention to the study of the material world:

> Erkundung des Stofflichen und Sinnlichen war ihm sein All und Eines geworden. (XI, 4)

Reinhart's physical studies had brought on a case of eye-trouble, a symbolical representation of the restricted nature of his purely scientific outlook, and he decided to take a vacation to rest up and cure his eyes. At the same time, to liven things up a bit, he proposed to carry out an interesting experiment suggested by an epigram from Logau, namely to find a girl who when kissed would laugh and blush simultaneously:

---

[31] *Ermatinger* II, 275. Book one of *Der Grüne Heinrich* was written in 1851. Book four, in which the philosophy of freewill was developed, was written in 1855.

> Wie willst du weisze Lilien zu roten Rosen machen?
> Küsz eine weisze Galathee: sie wird errötend lachen.
>   (XI, 5) [32]

The epigram is the clue to an understanding of both the marital-ethical and philosophical motifs. It is clearly the "formula for the perfect girl":

> The epigram thus becomes ... a formula for the perfect girl. Such a girl must have the freedom of spirit and the capacity to laugh; she must be thoroughly *aware* (author's italics) of what she does and feels, so as not to be bound to the earth like an animal. But she must also be able to blush—that is, she must not have lost contact with the world of instinct, of feeling; and her experiences must not be so intellectualized that she can forget that they touch her own self intimately in body as well as soul. If by laughing she shows herself to be a human being and a free spirit, she proves by blushing that she is capable of feeling as a woman. *She must be able to recognize her nature and submit to the laws of her sex.* (my italics) [33]

And the perfect girl in turn reflects the ideal philosophy. Implicit in her "freedom of spirit and ... capacity to laugh," while at the same time submitting consciously "to the laws of her sex," is that peculiar combination of determinism and moral idealism that went to form Keller's ideal of intellectual freedom.

After several romantic encounters in which either only the sensuous or only the moral aspect of the epigram was fulfilled, Reinhart finally met the heroine Lucie. Lucie was Reinhart's counterpart in every respect. She possessed the innate conservatism of woman and was quite angry with him for the essentially *unsittlich* nature of his experiment.[34] She was enlightened and aware of the moral law. Her enlightened outlook is apparent both from the descriptive sentence: "Nicht nur vom Abglanz der Abendsonne, sondern auch von einem hellen inneren Lichte war die ziervolle Dame dermaszen erleuchtet..."[35] and from

---

[32] The epigram in the form used here had been changed by Lessing; *errötet* was changed to *errötend* to show that the inner reaction occurred simultaneously.

[33] Priscilla Kramer, *The Cyclical Method of Composition in Gottfried Keller's Sinngedicht*, p. 52.

[34] "... rötete sich ihr Gesicht in anmutigem Zorn, und plötzlich stand sie auf und sagte mit verdächtigem Lächeln": ... (XI, 41).

[35] This sentence appeared in the first description of Lucie. Both Edgar Neis and Max Hochdorf (cf. appendix pp. 150, 154) interpreted the sentence to mean that Lucie possessed "*Geistesfreiheit*."

her very name Lucie, or its shortened form, Lux; light always symbolized intellectual clarity for Keller.[36] Lucie's awareness of the moral law is evident from the fact that her house was filled with the literature of all tongues and all ages and that her especial hobby was the reading of biographies. Her interest in all intellectual achievement resembles Heinrich Lee's concern with history in his study of the moral law, and her interest in people's lives reveals her desire to understand human nature, the key to an understanding of the moral law. Lucie's enlightenment was apparent even to Reinhart:

> Des Fräuleins ausführliche und etwas scharfe Beredsamkeit über die Schwächen einer Nachbarin und Genossin ihres Geschlechtes hatte ihn anfänglich befremdet und ein fast unweiblich kritisches Wesen befürchten lassen. *Indem er sich aber der Lieblingsbücher erinnerte*, die er kurz vorher gesehen, glaubte er in dieser Art mehr die Gewohnheit zu erkennen, *in der Freiheit über den Dingen zu leben*, die Schicksale zu verstehen und jegliches bei seinem Namen zu nennen. (XI, 55) (my italics)

Attractive, *sittlich*, and enlightened as she is, Lucie appears at first glance to be both the perfect woman and the symbol of intellectual freedom, and a cursory reading of the *Sinngedicht* might lead one to believe with Ermatinger that Lucie was from the beginning "die weibliche Verkörperung dieses Idealzustandes von Lust und Sitte" (I, 593). Indeed, evidence can be found to support this view. Reinhart began his "Augenkur" in Lucie's home, a symbolical statement that the overbold male was seeking help from womanly *Sittlichkeit* and that determinism was seeking a cure in the realm of moral idealism. Furthermore, in the course of his lengthy discussions with Lucie, Reinhart regained his faith in the moral law, evidenced both in the fact that his eye ailment was gradually cured and in a pregnant symbolism at the story's end:

> Reinhart nannte später seine schöne Frau . . . Lux und indem er das Wortspiel fortsetzte, die Zeit, da er sie noch nicht gekannt hatte . . . ante lucem, vor Tagesanbruch. (XI, 380)

The period before he became enlightened and regained his belief in the moral law had been "before the dawn."

Thus it would seem that only the determinist, Reinhart,

---
[36] For a discussion of Keller's symbolism, cf. pp. 113-114 in this study.

needed to be set aright, a conclusion which led Max Hochdorf to assert that the *Sinngedicht* was an expression of Keller's earlier romantic belief in freewill, rather than of the determinism of his maturity.[37]

The fact of the matter is, however, that this is not at all the case and that Keller had once again resorted to what scholars agree was a consistent practice of his later works, camouflage, to keep his basic ideas from being bandied about by critics.[38] It will be recalled that the story was built around the epigram, and that the perfect woman had to be able to conform to its requirements. Lucie was not this perfect woman at the outset; she was able to meet the requirements of the epigram only at the end of the story after learning to respect Reinhart's views. It must now be clearly understood that their conversations had been far from one-sided. Reinhart as a typical man had admitted to no weakness and was just as convinced that Lucie's ideas were without merit as Lucie was certain that Reinhart's outlook was circumscribed, with the result that there had been a contest of ideas in which each had learned to respect the views of the other. Such an exchange of ideas was possible as Reinhart had not defended determinism against idealism but a thesis born of his masculine nature, that an intelligent, educated man could take an uneducated girl for his wife and still have a successful marriage; and in connection with this view, Reinhart had himself been an exponent of enlightenment. Each of his heroes sought to educate his beloved (Regine, the Baroness, Zambo) to a free outlook. For example, Don Correa enjoyed watching "wie von Tag zu Tag das Verständnis heller aufging und die junge Frau mit dem Lichte menschlichen Bewusztseins erfüllte"; and when he finally asked her whether she would have given him her hand "ehedem (du) deine Freiheit gekannt hättest," Zambo had answered by looking him "ernst und hochaufgerichtet in die Augen und gab ihm mit freier und sicherer Bewegung die rechte Hand" (XI. 314).

Reinhart had taught as well as learned, so that a process of *mutual* education had followed during which each had come to appreciate the views of the other. Had Lucie not learned to respect Reinhart's views, she certainly could not have learned to

---

[37] Max Hochdorf, *Zum geistigen Bilde von Gottfried Keller*, p. 12.

[38] Keller was vigorously denounced by numerous critics for his alleged materialism and determinism.

love him. Thus the development of the action supports Priscilla Kramer's contention[39] that Lucie was not the perfect woman to start with, but was, as Reinhart had sensed, too arbitrary in her outlook. Lucie had concerned herself with the moral law to the extent that she had submerged her womanhood. Her moral idealism had stood for an arbitrary freedom. Only after she had reacquired her long neglected womanly feelings in her love for Reinhart was Lucie able to conform to the requirements of the epigram; only then was she able to kiss him, while quite unconsciously laughing and blushing at the same time.

Neither Reinhart nor Lucie was at the outset perfect as a person or as the embodiment of a philosophical attitude. Each had first to win from the other what he was lacking. Reinhart learned decorum and regained his belief in the moral law. Lucie regained her womanly feelings and her belief in natural law. Both characters came to possess the insight which revealed that man was a creature of nature but with a law of his own, and hence both came to possess the moral freedom to act in accordance with that law. They became intellectually free. Furthermore, their marriage symbolized a fusion of determinism with moral idealism, of a belief in natural law with a belief in moral law, thus forming Keller's ideal of intellectual freedom.

The *Prolog zur Schillerfeier in Bern* (1859), while a tribute to Schiller's lofty conviction that ideal beauty alone led to morality, was also a mighty hymn to intellectual freedom since Keller attributed to *Schönheit* all the characteristics of *Einsicht*.[40] Beauty, like insight, was a dynamic quality which was developing toward perfection:

> Die (Schönheit) jugendlich, ein schäumender Alpenstrom,
> Die erste Kraft im jähen Felsprung übt,
> Dann aber sich vertieft im klaren See
> Und auferstehend aus der Purpurnacht
> Dem Meer der Ewigkeit und der Vollendung
> Kraftvoll mit breiter Flut entgegenzieht.
> (I, 271)

---

[39] Priscilla Kramer, *op. cit.*, p. 52.
[40] *Einsicht* it will be remembered, referred to the intellectual clarity which led to freewill (GH XIX, 69); (cf. also p. 63 of the present study). Had Keller not made the clear distinction between *Schönheit* and *Freiheit* in the *Prolog*, it would not have been grossly incorrect to have identified *Schönheit* itself with intellectual freedom.

Beauty preferred to dwell among moral people and clear thinkers. It revealed the world as it truly was. It penetrated to the core of life and gave life new meaning,[41] happiness,[42] freedom from coincidence,[43] purposefulness,[44] and inner accord:[45]

> Die Schönheit ist's, die Friedrich Schiller lehrt,
> Die süsz und einfach da am liebsten wohnt,
> Wo edle Sitte sie dem Reiz vermählt
> *Und der Gedanken strenge Zucht gedeiht!*
> Die Schönheit ist's, die nicht zum Ammenmärchen
> Die Welt uns wandelt und das Menschenschicksal,
> Zaghaft der Wahrheit heil'gem Ernst entfliehend—
> Nein! die das Leben tief im Kern ergreift
> Und in Feuer taucht, draus es geläutert
> In *unbeirrter* Freude Glanz hervorgeht,
> *Befreit von Zufall, einig in sich selbst*—
> Und klar hinwandelnd wie des Himmels Sterne!
> (I, 271, *Gesammelte Gedichte*) (my italics)

Beauty subordinated the individual peculiarities of men, so that, in complete freedom, they were united as a whole:

> Dasz sie (die Schönheit) das Eigenart'ge und Besondre
> Was uns beschränkt, frei mit der Welt verbinde ... (I, 269)

Beauty gave power and harmony to thought and prevented the twisted thoughts which are the seeds of unfree acts. Beauty alone led to the highest freedom and maintained that freedom:

> Zur höchsten Freiheit führt allein die Schönheit;
> Die echte Schönheit nur erhält die Freiheit,
> Dasz diese nicht vor Jahren stirbt.
> Vollkraft und Ebenmasz gibt sie dem Denken,
> Schon eh es sinnlich sich zur Tat verkörpert,
> Und knechtisch ist das unschön Miszgestalte,
> Im Keim verborgener Gedanken schon.
> (I, 269)

The highest freedom was of course Schiller's *moralische Freiheit*.[46] Thus, beauty alone led to and safeguarded moral conduct.

---

[41] "draus es geläutert ... hervorgeht"
[42] "in unbeirrter Freude"
[43] "Befreit von Zufall"
[44] "klar hinwandelnd wie des Himmels Sterne"
[45] "einig in sich selbst"
[46] Schiller's *Aesthetische Briefe*, in which his theory of ideal beauty was developed, presumed Kant's *moralische Freiheit* to be the highest goal of man. Keller undoubtedly realized that Schiller's *Freiheit*, based on a Kantian dualism, differed from his own. Cf. Herbert Reichert: *A Comparison of the Philosophies of Schiller and Keller*, Monatshefte, April, 1947. Cf. also pp. 129-132 in this study.

Leading scholars have recognized the identity of *Schönheit* and intellectual clarity. Hans Dünnebier linked *Schönheit* with Feuerbach's term, *Selbsterkenntnis*:

> ..... die sittlichen Forderungen sind echt Feuerbachische . . . Selbsterkenntnis ist die Grundlage alles Glückes . . .[47]

Emil Ermatinger interpreted *Schönheit* as "freie Klarheit" which led to "sittliche Freiheit."[48]

It is evident that *Schönheit* as used in the *Prolog* is comparable with intellectual clarity and beauty's "Vollendung" with universal enlightenment. Once again, Keller had been stating his conviction that intellectual clarity alone led to moral freedom and that enlightenment alone preserved that freedom.[49]

All of the stories of *Die Leute von Seldwyla* reveal Keller's predominant concern with intellectual freedom; but with the possible exception of *Spiegel das Kätzchen*, his attitude is most clearly shown in *Das Verlorene Lachen* (1872). The relation of this *Novelle* to the *Sinngedicht* has already been shown by Ermatinger:

> In dem "Verlorenen Lachen" nehmen die Namen Jukundus und Justine den Zweiklang Lust und Recht wieder auf, und eine wahrhaft glückliche Ehe zwischen den beiden wird erst möglich auf der Grundlage sittlicher, das heiszt politischer und religiöser Klarheit. (*Ermatinger* I, 593)

The theme of the story is that lack of clarity on the part of both characters leads them into difficulties from which new insight finally rescues them. Justine had to rise above her confused religious ideas. Jukundus had to free himself from naive conceptions about the nature of his fellow-men. At the end of the

---

[47] Hans Dünnebier, *op. cit.*, p. 166. As human nature and the moral law were the object of Keller's interest, *Selbsterkenntnis* is identical with intellectual clarity. To show, however, that the concept was not originally borrowed from Feuerbach, one need only recall the letter of 1837, the diary notation of 1838, or the poem *Erkenntnis*.

[48] I, 386. Ermatinger saw only the political and religious significance of "sittliche Freiheit":
> Vorüber sind die halbbewuszten Tage unsicheren Werdens und dämonischen Ringens. Klar und frei gilt es ins Reich der Zukunft auszufahren. Diese freie Klarheit gibt nur die Schillersche Schönheit im Sinne eines harmonischen Gleichgewichtes zwischen Sinnlichkeit und Verstand, *den Ansprüchen des Einzelnen und denen der Gesamtheit.*
> (*Ermatinger* I, 386) (my italics)

Ermatinger, too, felt Keller was expressing Feuerbach's views:
> Und machtvoll und mutig ertönt wieder das humanistische Diesseitsevangelium Feuerbachs: Die Schönheit ist's . . . (*Ermatinger* I, 386)

[49] Note how closely this statement of attitude parallels the diary notation of the youthful Keller that "geistige Selbständigkeit" alone preserved moral integrity.

story, the enlightened Jukundus voices his religious belief. The degree to which he expressed Keller's views is apparent from the fact that he has finally become enlightened, and that he speaks with great deliberation (*bedächtig*). Jukundus even went to the trouble of distinguishing between his "Gottesfurcht" and the "schwesterliche Liebe" of Justine:

> Denn sie besasz warmes religiöses Gefühl, aber sie war in Hinsicht auf göttliche Dinge viel zu neugierig und indiskret und hatte auch ein zu groszes persönliches Sicherheitsgefühl, um das haben zu können, was man in reinerem Sinne sonst unter Gottesfurcht verstanden hat. (VIII, 345)

The passage in question reads:

> Ich glaube, der Sache nach, habe ich wohl etwas wie Gottesfurcht, indem ich Schicksal und Leben gegenüber, keine Frechheit zu äuszern fähig bin. Ich glaube nicht vorlegen zu können, dasz es überall und selbstverständlich gut gehe, sondern fürchte, dasz es hie und da schlimm ablaufen könne, und hoffe, dasz es sich dann doch zum bessern wenden werde. Zugleich ist mir bei allem, was ich auch ungesehen und von Andern ungewuszt tue und denke, das Ganze der Welt gegenwärtig, *das Gefühl*,[50] *als ob zuletzt Alle um Alles wüszten* und kein Mensch über eine wirkliche Verborgenheit seiner Gedanken und Handlungen verfügen oder seine Torheiten und Fehler nach Belieben totschweigen könnte. Das ist einem Teil von uns angeboren, dem andern nicht, ganz abgesehen von allen Lehren der Religion. Ja, die stärksten Glaubenseiferer und Fanatiker haben gewöhnlich gar keine Gottesfurcht, sonst würden sie nicht so leben und handeln, wie sie es wirklich tun.
>
> Wie nun dieses Wissen Aller um Alles möglich und beschaffen ist, weisz ich nicht; aber ich glaube es handelt sich um *eine ungeheuere Republik des Universums, welche nach einem einzigen und ewigen Gesetze lebt und in welcher schlieszlich alles gemeinsam gewuszt wird. Unsere heutigen kurzen Einblicke lassen eine solche Möglichkeit mehr ahnen als je;* denn noch nie ist die innere

---

[50] Keller discussed such religious feelings in *Der Grüne Heinrich* in connection with Green Henry's "inniges und tiefes Gefühl der Gottheit" (XVIII, 134). Keller stated that *Gefühle* which "oft ganz nah an das Gebiet der Ideen streifen" could be transmitted by inheritance "in einzelnen Familien wie in ganzen Stämmen." (So closely were these feelings related to thoughts that Keller continued his discussion in terms of "angeborene Gedanken.") Keller realized that "das Angeborene eines Gedankens noch kein Beweis für dessen Erfüllung ist, sondern ein blozses Ergebnis der langen Fortpflanzung in den Geschlechtsfolgen sein kann," as was seen in the fact that the Russians had a basic "Unterwürfigkeitstrieb," whereas the English possessed a "Freiheitsgefühl" which was "physisch angeboren." Nevertheless, these *Gefühle* or *angeborene Gedanken* were the greatest reality that man knew as they were the "Frucht tausendjähriger Wachstumes" and thus reflected most closely the inner force in history. Keller's belief in inherited feelings or idea-feelings remained with him throughout his life; he still commented in *Martin Salander* that Martin was unaware that his daughters had inherited their "fixe Ideen" from him (*Hertz* VIII, 264).

Wahrheit des Wortes so fühlbar gewesen, das in diesem Buche steht: In meines Vaters Hause sind viele Wohnungen! (VIII, 346) (my italics)

Here then is Keller's admission of faith: an irrational belief in the eventual realization of universal enlightenment and in a millennium when the whole universe would be run according to the one moral law. Moral freedom based on enlightenment was still the rosy goal of the future.

The most outstanding of the *Züricher Novellen* is generally conceded to be *Der Landvogt von Greifensee* (1877). In subtle fashion, this *Novelle* also extols the ideal of intellectual freedom,[51] since the hero achieves happiness through conscious renunciation. Salomon Landolt, *Landvogt* of the district of Greifensee in a bygone century, was for various reasons unable to marry any one of five young women with whom he had fallen deeply in love. Each love-affair brought with it new heart-ache but also new insight, and finally Landolt wisely concluded that he was destined to remain single. Realization of his lot and subsequent obedience to the law of his being enabled Landolt to become a happy and successful man. The episode around which the story is centered reveals that his decision had been based on true enlightenment. Landolt invited all his former sweethearts to a party where he led them to believe they were to choose as his bride either his old housekeeper or a young servant girl—actually a house-boy in disguise. The ladies, with the possible exception of Figura Leu, showed themselves motivated by such selfish aims that Landolt and the reader could plainly see that none would have made a suitable mate. Thus, Landolt had been enlightened and had acted according to his needs; he had been intellectually free.

Keller devoted the entire first part of the story to descriptions and incidents which showed that Landolt was thoroughly enlightened. One is told immediately that he was renowned for his initiative and independence ("selbständiges Vorgehen").[52] Like Lucie,[53] his eyes were cool and steady, and betrayed the "innewohnenden Geist":

---

[51] Edgar Neis: *Romantik und Realismus in Gottfried Kellers Prosawerken*, p. 89. Neis recognized that the story was a defense of enlightenment. He used the term *Geistesfreiheit*.
[52] *Hertz* VI, 145.
[53] Cf. pp. 72-73.

> Die *hellen* braunen Augen blickten *frei, fest und den innewohnenden* Geist verratend, umher . . . (*Hertz* VI, 147) (my italics)

He remained calm and gentle while reconciling a child, incurably ill, to its impending death:

> So setzte sich Landolt, *ruhig seine Pfeife rauchend*, an das Bett und sprach zu ihm in so einfachen und treffenden Worten von der Hoffnungslosigkeit seiner Lage, von der Notwendigkeit sich zu fassen und eine kleine Zeit zu leiden, aber auch von der sanften Erlösung durch den Tod und der seligen *wechsellosen Ruhe*. (*Hertz* VI, 153) (my italics)

By means of this symbolism, Keller revealed that Landolt possessed the "ruhige feste Gleichmut" which not even contact with the deepest mysteries of life can disturb. Furthermore, Landolt's conception of death as "wechsellose Ruhe," Keller's own view, showed that he had come to a true understanding of things.

Not only did Landolt retain his quiet self-possession in critical moments, but he responded to conventionally embarrassing situations with an easy humorous laugh—another symbol of an enlightened outlook.[54] Also, in his capacity as judge he showed remarkable insight. Using entirely unorthodox methods, he delved into the heart of each case and dealt out true justice without concern for technicalities (*Hertz* VI, 228-234). Like Keller, a dilettante artist of the better kind, Landolt emphasized in his paintings the inner harmony and *Ruhe* in nature:

> Seine Malkapelle bot einen ungewöhnlichen, reichhaltigen Anblick . . . so mannigfaltig die Schildereien waren, die sich den Augen darboten, so leuchtete doch aus allen derselbe kühne und zugleich *still harmonische Geist*. Der unablässige Wandel, das Aufglimmen und Verklingen der *innerlich ruhigen Natur* schienen nur die wechselnden Akkorde desselben Tonstückes zu sein. (*Hertz* VI, 211) (my italics)

Despite the emotions which would normally arise at the sight of one's former sweethearts, Landolt had been able to consider them calmly without pangs of memory or remorse: "Mit zufriedenem Auge prüfte er, verglich . . ." (*Hertz* VI, 227).[55] He had invited them without malice: "Mit einem warmen Glücksgefühl sah er sie versammelt" (*Hertz* VI, 236).

---

[54] *Hertz* VI, 152, 155, etc. The significance of laughter as an indication of enlightenment was brought out in both the *Sinngedicht* and in *Das Verlorene Lachen*.

[55] As author of the story Keller had not been so noble, since he placed all of the women but Figura Leu in an unfavorable light.

It is interesting to note that this is the first *Novelle* in the *Zürich* cycle in which Keller dealt with the historical facts rather freely. More and more, scholars are coming to the conclusion that the work was largely autobiographical. Keller, in his secretive way, apparently wanted to show that his bachelordom was a result of enlightened renunciation.[56]

The revised version of *Der Grüne Heinrich* (1880) has been felt by some scholars to contain a changed *Weltanschauung*. They cite as evidence a new episode, inserted directly after Heinrich's monologue on freewill, in which the resolute actions of a spider rebuilding its web again and again in the face of almost insuperable obstacles, seem to Heinrich startlingly similar to the actions of a free being:

> Hierüber erstaunte ich nicht wenig; denn eine solche Entschluszfähigkeit in dem winzigen Gehirnchen erhob sich beinahe zu der menschlichen Willensfreiheit, die ich behauptete, oder sie zog diese zu sich herunter in den Bereich des blinden Naturgesetzes, des leidenschaftlichen Antriebes. Um diesem zu entrinnen, erhöhte ich sofort meine sittlichen Ansprüche, da es beim Bauen von Luftschlössern auf ein Mehr oder Weniger an Unkosten ja niemals ankommt. Ob auch Luftschlösser sich verwirklichen oder ob sie mindestens dazu dienen, eine goldene Mittelstrasze zu schützen, wie das römische Castrum einst den Heerweg, wird wohl das Geheimnis einer Erfahrung sein, welches erworbene Bescheidenheit nicht immer preisgibt. (VI, 20, *Der Grüne Heinrich*, revised.)

Had they wished, these scholars might also have mentioned that in the revised version Keller omitted the passages dealing with *Einsicht* and no longer used the word *Wahrheit* to refer to the work of the great exponent of human freewill, Schiller. Does this mean then that Keller in his later years gave up his belief in intellectual freedom as the goal of humanity?

In the first place, if the passage quoted above is to indicate a change in attitude, then the concept in question, "menschliche Willensfreiheit," must have been basic to Keller's earlier attitude as expressed in the original *Grüner Heinrich*, and must be comparable to the idea of freewill developed there, namely, the freewill Lys and the mature Heinrich possessed: *Willensfreiheit* must mean intellectual freedom. But this is apparently not the case since intellectual freedom was a recognitional freewill,

---

[56] It would seem, since the subject matter bordered on his favorite theme and the problem of his own life, that Keller had chosen to subordinate historical fact to his ideal and incidentally to vindicate himself.

the acquisition of which enabled one to act from inner necessity like the spider,[57] while *Willensfreiheit* stood in opposition to the necessary actions of the spider and seemed to refer to an arbitrary freewill. If this be so, if *Willensfreiheit* does not coincide with Keller's conception of *Freiheit* in 1855, then obviously the questioning of such *Willensfreiheit* is irrelevant to a discussion of a change in attitude. Keller indirectly confirms this hypothesis in a sentence immediately following the spider episode. He used a metaphor to show that the *Willensfreiheit* under question was not his idea of true freedom:

> So war ich also mit dem glänzenden Schwerte der Willensfreiheit bewaffnet, ohne aber ein Fechter zu sein. (VI, 20)

Heinrich had freewill without being free. His concept was still too arbitrary to be usable.

If, on the other hand, *Willensfreiheit* is taken to coincide with Keller's *Freiheit* of 1855, then its questioning again means nothing since Heinrich, at the end of the revised version, did attain a *Willensfreiheit* comparable to intellectual freedom; after he had disavowed belief in immortality and a personal God, Heinrich became convinced (and Keller with him, as will be shown) that he had finally acquired *völlige Geistesfreiheit*:

> ich müszte mich nachträglich selber der Frivolität zeihen, wenn ich nicht annehmen könnte, dasz jene verblümte und spaszhafte Art eigentlich nur die Hülle der völligen Geistesfreiheit gewesen sei, die ich mir endlich erworben habe. (VI, 236)

The correctness of his conviction is shortly thereafter revealed in his relations with Judith.[58]

To eliminate any possible doubt about what Keller meant by *völlige Geistesfreiheit*, whether intellectual clarity or full in-

---

[57] The action of the spider was for Keller by no means antithetical to the actions of an enlightened human being. In both cases the action is born of inner necessity. Keller always insisted that man act from inner necessity. The only difference between the spider and man lay in Keller's conviction (cf. Herder and Schiller) that man was able to misconstrue his inner necessity and had to be intellectually free before he was able to be himself at all times (XIX, 62). Keller subtly identified the spider and Heinrich a few pages further on after the meditations on Schiller's life and works: Heinrich in adversity thought of the spider and decided there was for him also nothing else to do but try again (VI, 42).

[58] Here again Keller obscured his attitude toward freewill by having the priest laugh at Heinrich's assertion and comment, "Geistesfreiheit, Frivolität! Da zappelt der Fisch wieder an der langen Schnur und hält sich für einen Luftspringer!" Also, by having Heinrich become "ärgerlich, dasz ich dem humoristischen Fliegenfänger nun doch wieder ins Garn gefallen . . ." However, Keller portrays the priest most unsympathetically as a fanatical deist and would-be humorist, so that, when one considers the subsequent Judith scenes, it is clear that Keller had not changed his stand.

tellectual freedom, we may again turn our attention from terms to actions. Just as Lys showed what Keller meant by freewill in the original version, Judith shows what he meant in the revised version. Judith is endowed with an enlightened insight which enables her to subjugate the lower passions and heed the law of her destiny, the moral law.

In the new ending to the story, Judith returns from America thoroughly mature and enlightened:

> An dem Gesichte hatten die zehn Jahre keine andere Veränderung bewirkt, als dasz es selbstbewuszter geworden ... und eher veredelt als entstellt war. Erfahrung und Menschenkenntnis lagerten um Stirn und Lippen ... (VI, 312)

When she sees Heinrich for the first time in many years, her facial expression reveals her inner composure, reveals that she has acquired the "feste ruhige Gleichmut" which comes with enlightenment:

> Aber gleichzeitig überflog eine unverstellte und doch *unbeschreiblich milde* Freude ihr schönes Gesicht; (VI, 312) (my italics)

The insight which came from ten years in the new world has developed her original, natural goodness into a mature, moral sense:

> Da sah ich, dasz dieses Weib, das die Meere durchschifft, sich in einer neuen werdenden Welt herumgetrieben und zehn Jahre älter geworden, zarter und besser war als in der Jugend und in der stillen Heimat. (VI, 314)

Judith's description of her life in America further shows her enlightened understanding and moral nature. She had purchased a large tract of land which she allowed the colonists to work rent-free. But while she had their best interests at heart and showed the zeal of the aged Faust, she was not filled with any unrealistic notions; and when her generosity was abused, she took back her land and paid the colonists by the day. Modestly, she withdrew from the community after its success was assured.

Judith is and has been in love with Heinrich:

> Du liegst mir einmal im Blut und ich habe dich nie vergessen, da jeder Mensch etwas haben musz, woran er hängt. (VI, 318)

She returns to Switzerland only because she has heard he was in need. She is still a beautiful, vigorous woman, and near him every fiber of her physical self yearns "to take what the world calls happiness and become (with Heinrich) man and wife." But instead she abstains. She abstains consciously because her wide experience has shown her that conventional happiness is often a mirage, and because she knows that Heinrich would eventually regret such a marriage. In other words, she knows that her present limited happiness near him is the maximum she is destined to have, and that seeking more than her alloted share will only bring her unhappiness. Thus, she consciously renounces what a less enlightened person might have felt was "inner necessity" so that she may obey the true dictates of the moral law. She knows her destiny and follows it:

> Sieh, und nun könnten wir hier auch das Glück von Gottes Tisch nehmen, was die Welt das Glück nennt, und uns zu Mann and Frau machen! Aber wir wollen uns nicht krönen! Wir wollen jener Krone entsagen und dafür des Glückes um so sicherer bleiben, das uns jetzt, in diesem Augenblicke, beseligt; denn ich fühle, dasz du jetzt auch glücklich und zufrieden bist.... du bist noch jung Heinrich und kennst dich selber nicht. Aber abgesehen hievon, glaube mir, solange wir so sind, wie jetzt in dieser Stunde, wissen wir was wir haben! Was wollen wir denn mehr? (VI, 323)

Heinrich is aware that her action is the result of her wide experience:

> Ich begann zu fühlen und verstehen, was sie bewegte; sie mochte zu viel von der Welt gesehen und geschmeckt haben, um einen vollen und ganzen Glück zu trauen. (VI, 324)

The importance Keller placed on Judith's renunciation is implicit in the chapter heading: *Der Tisch Gottes*. To sum up, it is clear that Judith, in her conscious abstention based on her deep insight into life and human nature is a female counterpart of Salomon Landolt and a symbol of intellectual freedom.

Interestingly enough, Max Hochdorf, the scholar who felt that Keller was a determinist, recognized that Judith was a symbol of Keller's continued belief in freewill. Hochdorf was broadminded enough to admit that the ideas expressed at the end of the revised *Grüner Heinrich* did not fit in with his thesis of naturalism, and compared the revised version with Ibsen's *Doll House* to show, by contrast with Nora's irresolute actions, Judith's great *Willensfreiheit*:

> Eine von der Uebersättigung enttäuschte Frau sucht bei Ibsen die Einsamkeit, eine noch verlangende Frau verzichtet bei Keller.

Bei Keller ist es also die ungeheure Willensfreiheit, die triumphiert. Während Heinrich und Judith den Bezirk ihrer Seelenfreiheit abstecken, öffnet sich die Welt rings um sie sehr weit. Was diese beiden Menschenkinder wollen, ist wie der Wille, den sich alle Menschenkinder, denen ein gleiches Schicksal begegnet, auch aneignen sollten. Aus einer wirklichen Weltanschauung scheint der Wille von Judith und Heinrich herzustammen.[59]

Just what Hochdorf meant by *Willensfreiheit* need not concern us here. The important fact is that a scholar who believed that Keller was a naturalist recognized that the revised *Grüner Heinrich* was not a tribute to determinism, as the questioning of *Willensfreiheit* in the spider episode seemed to imply.

A further indication that the revised *Grüner Heinrich* was not an abnegation of *Freiheit* is apparent from the fact that the *Sinngedicht*, though conceived for the most part in the 1850's, was not put into written form until 1881, a year after *Der Grüne Heinrich* was revised. In order to defend his thesis (after Hochdorf) that Keller gradually became a determinist after 1860, Edgar Neis was forced to conclude that all of the stories in the *Sinngedicht*, because of their vigorous defense of enlightenment, were conceived before 1860.[60] Nevertheless, the *Sinngedicht* must be allowed to represent Keller's attitude in 1881 as well as his attitude of 1855-1860. For, if a changed attitude toward life had actually caused a change in the revised *Grüner Heinrich*, it would by rights have caused an alteration in the plan of the *Sinngedicht*. If an ostensible revision is significant for *Weltanschauung* in the one case, the lack of revision should be equally significant in the other. One may conclude, then, that the pointed questioning of freewill in the revised *Grüner Heinrich* did not reflect a significant change in Keller's attitude.

The question still remains unanswered, however, why Keller went to so much trouble to disguise his views. If he did not wish to indicate a change of attitude, why did he introduce the spider episode, leave out the passages on *Einsicht*, attribute the remaining speeches on freewill to Heinrich solely as a character, and in general carefully dissociate himself from Heinrich's views?

---

[59] Max Hochdorf, *Zum Geistigen Bilde von Gottfried Keller*, p. 78. Cf. app., p. 151.
[60] *Op. cit.*, p. 88, Cf. fn. 51.

The answer lies in the generally recognized fact that Keller through the years became ever more unwilling to reveal himself to the masses and have his innermost ideas bandied about.[61] Already in 1846 he pondered the matter in "An das Herz":

>Schau, wie sie verletzen　　　Keiner putzt die Schuhe,
>Dir das Hausrecht stets!　　　Keiner sieht sich um!
>Fühllos auf und nieder,　　　Staubig brechen Alle
>Polternd, lärmend gehts!　　　Dir ins Heiligtum;
>　　　　(XIV, 247, *Nachgelassene Gedichte*)

After 1855 he became more subtle in his technics and symbolism so that even scholars were long unaware of many of his basic views. The continuation of his desire to reveal himself only to a select few is apparent in the parable of the fisherman, written in 1881. At first the fisherman had followed the advice: "Wenn du Menschen fischen willst, so muszt du dein Herz an die Angel stecken, dann beiszen die an!" But when this procedure led to nothing but bad luck, he changed his tactics (concealed his views), and then he was eminently successful:

> Da war der Fischer betrübt. Allein bald wurde es ihm so leicht zu Muth, dasz er auf die wilde See hinaus fuhr und die Menschenfische zu Tausenden mit dem Netz fing, und er war nun ihr Herr und schlug sie auf die Köpfe.[62]

Keller was especially loath to reveal himself when in a bad humor; and if ever Keller was vexed, it was in the winter of 1879 when he wanted to begin work on the fourth volume of the revised version containing the discussion on freewill. Conditions in general depressed him as revealed in the melancholy poem "Land im Herbste" (1879):

>Das alte Lied, wo ich auch bliebe,
>Von Mühsal und Vergänglichkeit!
>Ein wenig Freiheit, wenig Liebe
>Und um das Wie der arme Streit!
>　　(I, 73, *Gesammelte Gedichte*)[63]

He lost one good friend after another: "Ein Altersgenosse nach dem andern wird kampfesunfähig oder segelt gar von dannen."[64]

---

[61] Critics attacked Keller mercilessly. R. Weber in the introduction to the *Poetische Nationalliteratur der deutschen Schweiz*, Vol. III, 1867, felt that the *Neuere Gedichte* contained "groben Realismus, sarkastischen Witz, verbitterten Humor und eklige Frivolität."

[62] *Nachgelassene Schriften und Dichtungen*, ed. by Baechtold, p. 335. Max Hochdorf recognized the importance of the parable. Cf. app., p. 151.

[63] Keller wrote to Storm in 1882 that the stanza referred solely to political conditions (*Ermatinger* III, 408).

[64] Cf. Ackerknecht's biography, p. 329.

The winter of 1879 was bitterly cold and he complained that his dwelling "sich als unträtabel erweise," and that Regula was so anxious to save firewood that "er friere sogar beim Essen ein und komme nicht mehr an eine zusammenhängende Schreibarbeit."[65] When he finally managed to get to work the following spring, his mood was such that he was less willing than ever to be exposed to the attacks of the critics.

Keller's last novel *Martin Salander* (1886) was a bitter depiction of the political corruption in Switzerland, following the adoption of a more democratic constitution in 1869. His vigorous condemnation of the excrescences of democratic rule might in itself appear to indicate a change in his optimistic *Weltanschauung,* but it will be recalled that his optimism had never been rooted in the present; bitterness over existing conditions did not necessarily imply a loss of faith in the future. The fact is, *Martin Salander* reaffirms wholeheartedly Keller's belief in the eventual, universal acquisition of intellectual freedom. A sharp distinction is made between present and future, and hope for Switzerland is seen in the enlightened outlook of the younger generation.

Leading scholars have expressed the conviction that Keller's optimism for the future remained unaltered in *Martin Salander.* Emil Ermatinger stated in his biography (1916): "Und dennoch darf man nicht von der Verurteilung der Demokratie sprechen" (p. 641). And in 1933 Ermatinger stated:

> Auch hier ringen sich die Lebenszuversicht des Dichters und der Glaube an die gesunde Kraft seines Volkes schlieszlich an die Oberfläche.[66]

Gleichen-Russwurm had said in 1921:

> Seine letzte abschlieszende Arbeit, der Roman "Martin Salander" spiegelt diesen Zustand ("der heutige Schwindel") und manche Grämlichkeit des alternden Dichters breitet graue Farbenstimmung darüber, ja man könnte in dem Werk sogar eine veränderte Weltanschauung wahrnehmen, wenn nicht die Hoffnung auf bessere Zeit, der gesunde Optimismus den düsteren Himmel aufhellte und am Schlusz, wie ein Sonnenstrahl am Abend eines spätsommerlichen Regentages, durch die Wolken bräche.[67]

---

[65] *Ibid.,* p. 333.
[66] Emil Ermatinger, *Dichtung und Geistesleben der deutschen Schweiz,* p. 640.
[67] *Op. cit.,* p. 104.

Hans Kriesi discussed in detail the optimistic second half of the novel as Keller had planned it, and concluded:

> Aber nachdem er die volle Schale seines Pessimismus ausgegossen, wollte er auch der Hoffnung wieder Raum gönnen und seiner Heimat den Weg zeigen, der aus diesem Labyrinthe des Unglücks wieder hinausführte.[68]

To contrast present and future in *Martin Salander* and to show where his sympathies lay, Keller made use of a character symbolism similar to that used in the *Sinngedicht*. Martin Salander represented the benighted, older generation of Swiss who insisted on the immediate democratization of their government without regard to the traditions of the past, while his son Arnold symbolized the enlightened younger generation which believed self-government had to be arrived at in a more "organic" and "natural" fashion.

Martin's limitations were made clear. He was a business man with little education whose chief interest was to amass a fortune.[69] He had no knowledge of the moral forces in history and disposed of them with a snort: "Dimensionen und Bedingungswerte (der Geschichte)! Gras wachsen hören!" (*Hertz* VIII, 159). He was unaware of the lesson taught by a study of history that all worthwhile change evolved from inner necessity. To Arnold's argument that while political self-determination was the purpose of the nation, such self-determination in order to have lasting value had to be reached by a more natural procedure, Martin merely showed lack of understanding. He felt that Arnold was a reactionary: "Das ist doktrinaire Kritik!... er weisz, dasz ich ein Mann des Fortschrittes bin..." (*Hertz* VIII, 161). Ignorance as to the existence of the moral law also caused Martin to become upset by the corrupt conditions and to lose faith in the future. When Frau Marie referred to the situation as unexplainable, "Wir haben es mit einer unerklärten Unregelmäszigkeit zu tun," Martin had agreed:

> Es wird wohl so sein! es gibt dergleichen in der moralischen wie in der physischen Welt. (*Hertz* VIII, 232)

Arnold, on the other hand, was imbued with intellectual freedom. He was a well-educated scholar willing to assume his share

---

[68] Hans M. Kriesi, *Gottfried Keller als Politiker*, p. 233.

[69] Not for selfish reasons, to be sure, but to provide for his family. Martin was sincere, and tried to be a good husband and father.

THE BASIC CONCEPTS, 1849-1886 89

of the social burden. He was aware that history was dynamic and that its course was determined by inner forces. His keenest interest was to learn more about these "Bedingungswerte":

> ... die werdende Geschichte besser zu verstehen und ihre Dimensionen messen, ihre Bedingungswerte schätzen zu lernen. (*Hertz* VIII, 159)[70]

Arnold's historical studies had given him an unshakable optimism regarding the future, which indicates his awareness of the moral law. He was not shaken like Martin by the troubled state of affairs since he had seen in his study of the war with Burgundy that the Swiss had been "verwildert" before and had nevertheless continued to exist and improve.[71] Arnold's studies had also led him to believe that lasting progress[72] could be achieved only by obedience to natural law. Swiss politics were in such a sad state, he felt, because the liberal party, which had come into power, disregarded the basic law of natural evolution and arbitrarily reversed the entire governmental procedure of its predecessor:

> Es handle sich un einen bedächtigeren, beharrlicheren Ausbau des Ganzen ... (*Hertz* VIII, 160)

The means whereby the nation could best fulfill its purpose was to adhere to the laws of its being:

> Es sei ein Naturgesetz, dasz alles Leben, je rastloser es gelebt werde, um so schneller sich auslebe und ein Ende nähme, daher ... vermöge er es nicht gerade als ein zweckmäsziges Mittel zur Lebensverlängerung anzusehen, wenn ein Volk die letzte Konsequenz, deren Keim in ihm stecke, vor der Zeit zu Tode hetze und damit sich selbst. (*Hertz* VIII, 60)

Arnold's intellectual freedom is evident from his faith in progress and from his realization that the *Volk* had to obey the natural law of its being. At the end of the story, moreover, to dispel any remaining uncertainty as to Arnold's enlightenment, Keller availed himself of a symbolic picture. Arnold invited his friends to a party, and his choice was such that all of the "Teilnehmer waren gleichmäszig gebildet, wohlunterrichtet und auch lebendi-

---

[70] Both Heinrich Lee and Lucie had turned to a study of history in their search for the moral law.
[71] (*Hertz* VIII, 337). As Arnold is evidently Keller's mouthpiece, here is clear evidence of Keller's continued optimism for the future.
[72] I.e., action in accord with the moral law.

gen Geistes . . .." Their conversation contained "nicht ein unfreisinniges Wort!" All of the group possessed the tolerance which came from a recognition of the predetermined nature of things including the upward progress of mankind. Thus, they did not condemn evildoers more than to say:

> Was wollt Ihr? Dem Kerl ist sein Weg vorgezeichnet, er musz ihn laufen und wird seinem Lohn nicht entgehen!

To stress further the enlightenment of Arnold and his friends, Keller had Martin, even at this point, doubt the intellectual abilities of the group:

> Die haben, dachte er, nicht die Fähigkeit, auf einer Idee zu beharren;

But immediately Martin had to alter his decision:

> Aber ehe er den Verdacht besser ausspinnen konnte, bewegte sich die Unterhaltung *auf weiten freien Bahnen;* keiner tat sich als Lehrer oder Prophet hervor, und Phrasen wurden noch weniger laut; man sah nur, dasz es männliche Jünglinge seien, *die sich die Welt offen hielten.* (*Hertz* VIII, 350) (my italics)

After Keller had made sufficiently clear what Martin and Arnold stood for, he revealed in another symbolical picture his belief that Switzerland would be saved by the enlightened, younger generation. Martin had become infatuated with a beautiful but simple-minded girl Myrrha, whose true personality remained a mystery to him even after an acquaintanceship of several months. Martin thought Myrrha was the reincarnation of the classic harmony between form and intellect, though she was actually a symbol of the superficiality of the times. Martin was saved from making a fool of himself by Arnold, who recognized Myrrha for what she was worth a few minutes after having been introduced to her, and then "in kalter Ruhe" told his father what she was really like. Ermatinger explains the symbolism nicely:

> Er (Martin) ist die Verkörperung des demokratischen Volkes . . .
> . . . .
>
> die "klassische" Scheinschönheit der blödsinnigen Myrrha; ein sehr herbes Symbol für den gefährlichen Hang der Gründerzeit zum Aeuszerlichen und Prunkhaften . . . .
>
> in seinem Sohne Arnold endlich verkörpert sich das Geschlecht, das auf die politisch gestimmte Generation der sechziger und siebziger Jahre folgte. (*Ermatinger* I, 640)

Thus, Keller's last work expressed the same firm hope and belief that through intellectual freedom the ills of mankind would one day be remedied.

Looking over Keller's writings from 1849-1886, or better from 1837-1886, one realizes it would be folly to deny that Keller's *Weltanschauung* was not affected by such high points in his life as the association with Feuerbach and the political crises in Switzerland, and that Keller like many another poetic personality allowed his understanding of life first to be colored by emotion and then, later, when he had acquired a degree of inner security, to be guided by reason. But it would be equally difficult to deny that the striking element in his outlook was not so much the change wrought by Feuerbach or the unavoidable cooling off which happens in every human life, as it was the stubborn retention throughout of his belief in a purposeful universe and in an eventual millennium based on enlightenment and moral freedom. The concepts *Natur* and *Freiheit* remained practically unchanged throughout Keller's mature years and in their essential features differed little from *Natur* and *Freiheit* as conceived in his youth. From 1837-1886, *Natur* referred to tangible nature and the apparent order of her forms. Though the personal God of Keller's youth, who served as the first cause in the great teleological structure, was dismissed in 1849 (perhaps in 1845), Keller retained his belief in the purposeful and ordered state of nature, and merely shifted his veneration to an impersonal reason or to the system as a whole; the depth of his later faith revealed itself time and again, most clearly however in the religious conviction of the enlightened Jukundus who felt that the time would come when every one would know of everything and the world would be run according to one law. Before as after 1849, the essence of nature was *Ruhe,* and already in 1845 God seemed identified with the *Ruhe* in nature. Before as after 1849, man was a part of the great order and hope for his future was attributed to this fact. *Freiheit* from beginning to end referred to the goal toward which man was traveling, to the freedom to act in a necessary way and be oneself, to the moral discernment which came with enlightenment. The only change in connection with *Freiheit* was that after 1849 it was no longer the purpose of the law of time but of the moral law within the human organism.

Thus, *Natur* and *Freiheit* formed the basis of Keller's personal religion, of his *Weltanschauung.*

CHAPTER III

NATUR AND *FREIHEIT* IN THE MAJOR FIELDS OF KELLER'S THOUGHT

In order to show further the importance to Keller's thought of the concepts, *Natur* and *Freiheit*, and to see how strongly they colored his views beyond the realm of pure speculation, Keller's ideas on ethics, aesthetics, politics, and social relations will now be considered. The treatment is by no means exhaustive and seeks only to present sufficient evidence to demonstrate conclusively the influence exerted by the concepts in the different fields of *Weltanschauung*.

A. Ethics

In common with many other Swiss writers of his time, Keller had a tendency to be didactic, so that his ethical views appear in most of his works. Perhaps the clearest, brief statement of his ethics, however, is to be found in *Der Apotheker von Chamounix* (1852-60), which was a satire on Heinrich Heine and on romantic subjectivity in general.

In this work Keller mocked Heine for his unwillingness to recognize the ubiquitous law of nature:

> Fische zeugen keine Vögel
> Feigen wachsen nicht auf Disteln.
> Närr'sche Menschen, närr'sche Götter!
> Keiner kann aus seiner Haut!
> (XVi, 227, *Nachgelassene Gedichte*)

You are what you are, says Keller, and it is impossible to change the law of your own nature. Words and wishful thinking are of no avail:

> Aber lasz o Tor! dir sagen:
> Nichts auf Erden noch im Himmel
> Wird durch Worte je erzwungen;
> Was er ist, das gilt ein Jeder!
>
> *Gilt ein Jeder doch am Ende*
> *Und kein Jota mehr noch minder* ...
> (XVi, 239)   (author's italics)

Each man should be himself and do calmly ("ruhig") what inner necessity destined him to do:

> Jeder sei für sich ein Mann,
> Schöpfend aus des Guten Urquell!
> Was er kann, *mit innern Gluten,*
> Bring ers *ruhig* zu dem Ganzen.
> (XVi, 306)   (my italics)

Moral conduct was action born of inner necessity.

If one reflects for a moment on how the basic concepts figured in this ethical system, it becomes immediately apparent that *Natur* as the teleologic cosmos was of fundamental importance. For man was subject to the law of nature and was subject in particular, like fish and thistles, to the law of his own nature. In addition, since man was to draw from "des Guten Urquell" and yet to act only "mit innern Gluten," it is clear that the essence of morality was action in accord with inner law and hence in accord with the harmony of nature.

There are two facts which indicate that *Freiheit* also was a cornerstone of this system. The ideal man was to possess the unruffled serenity ("bring er's ruhig zu dem Ganzen") which in Keller's eyes came only with intellectual freedom; and he was to draw as best he could from the source of Good within himself, a feat which implied that he was an enlightened individual who understood himself and who had the power of moral discernment.

The importance of *Freiheit* to moral conduct was brought out very clearly in the scene, discussed earlier, between Ferdinand Lys and Heinrich Lee.[1] Lys, though unconventional, had been moral because he had the freewill to recognize his nature and to bring his principles and acts into accord with that nature, whereas Heinrich, despite the excellence of his intentions, had acted unethically because he had not understood himself sufficiently well to act from inner necessity. Blinded by the tenets of orthodox dogma, Heinrich had accused Lys of atheism and inconsistency, thereby precipitating the tragic duel.[2] Heinrich shows that an unenlightened person was not free to obey the moral law and even with the best of intentions was likely to violate the plan of nature and to be the cause of tragedy.

---
[1] Cf. pp. 65-68 in this study.
[2] XVIII, 241 (*Der Grüne Heinrich III*).

Keller's standard of moral conduct changed little throughout his life and always entailed the same combination of determinism and idealism. As a youth he had praised *die Freiheit*, "die, den der sie erkennt, keine schlechte Tat begehen läszt"[3] (1837), but had also said, "Der Mensch soll nicht tugendhaft sondern nur natürlich sein, und die Tugend wird von selbst kommen."[4] Whereas the diary notation of 1838 had insisted on *geistige Selbständigkeit*,[5] the poem, "Misztraue allem Auszerordentlichen" of the same year rejected any behavior that was not in agreement with nature.[6] Although a whole series of poems written in the 1840's defended *Freiheit*, the poem "Erkenntnis" contained the line, "Tu frei und offen was du . . . nicht kannst lassen."[7] As an older man Keller said the same. The *Prolog* of 1859 revealed that moral conduct was free, enlightened behavior which was nevertheless purposeful and regular as the stars.[8] *Martin Salander* (1886) showed that the moral salvation of the Swiss was to be found in the enlightened outlook of those young people who were aware both of natural law in general and of the moral law.[9] Keller's outlook was strikingly consistent, and in the persistence of the outlook one may discern the persistence of the basic concepts.

Natur and *Freiheit* also determined Keller's conception of evil. He was so convinced of the all-pervading goodness of nature that he consistently denied the possibility of a principle of evil. The only true force, he felt, was the moral force. In his lyrics of freedom he had proclaimed that nothing could stop the onward march to universal moral freedom[10] and later, in *Der Grüne Heinrich*, he had still insisted that there was no force of reaction and no principle of evil:

> So wenig die Physiker der Wärme gegenüber eine eigentümliche Kälte kennen, so wenig es dem Schönen gegenüber eine absolute dämonische Häszlichkeit gibt, wie die dualistischen Aesthetiker glauben, *so wenig wie es ein gehörntes und geschwänztes Prinzip des Bösen, einen selbstherrlichen Teufel gibt*, so wenig gibt es eine Reaktion, welche aus eigener innewohnender Kraft und nach

---

[3] *Ermatinger* II, 6. Cf. also pp. 34-39 in this study.
[4] *Ermatinger* II, 9. Cf. also pp. 34-39 in this study.
[5] *Ermatinger* II, 101. Cf. also pp. 39-40 in this study.
[6] XIII, 9. Cf. also p. 22 in this study.
[7] I, 45. Cf. also p. 25 in this study.
[8] Cf. pp. 75-77 in this study.
[9] Cf. pp. 87-91 in this study.
[10] Cf. pp. 47-48 in this study.

einem ursprünglichen Gesetze zu bestehen vermöchte. (XIX, 62, *Der Grüne Heinrich IV*) (my italics)

Keller conceived of evil as a growing pain of humanity. Like Herder and Schiller[11] he accepted the doctrine that man was progressing toward a state of perfection, and like them, he felt that evil resulted from man's temporary discordance with nature; man had left behind the state of involuntary nature and was progressing toward a voluntary acceptance of nature. Evil was no more than the reflection of humanity's intellectual infancy and would disappear forever when man, once again, returned to nature.

The doctrine that man was progressing from a necessary to a free perfection was never stated in a very connected fashion by Keller, except perhaps in the *Prolog* of 1859. His adherence to such a doctrine may nevertheless be noted from his constant admiration for the "natürliche" and "ursprüngliche Mensch,"[12] from his statement in *Der Grüne Heinrich* that most of mankind had left the state of pure nature and had already acquired a degree of enlightenment,[13] and from his everpresent belief that man was proceeding toward conscious morality and natural conduct. The following passage from the *Prolog* may be taken as a sincere expression of consistent attitude:

> Das ist das Wort! und mutig sag ich es:
> Vorüber sind die halbbewuszten Tage
> Unsichern Werdens und dämonischen Ringens!
> Und freudig sag' ich: Unserer Geschichten
> Sei nur das erste Halbteil nun getan!
> So gilt es auch, die andre schuld'ge Hälfte
> Mit unerschlaffter Hand heranzuführen,
> Dasz hell das Ende, das uns einst beschieden,
> *Sich in des Anfangs fernem Glanze spiegle*,
> Und dasz es heiszt: was diese werden konnten,
> Das haben sie voll Lebensmut erfüllt! (my italics)

Keller's ratiocination on the Jesuits illuminates his conception of the source of evil. Though there was no principle of evil, human progress could be retarded by dogmatic teachings, as these set up arbitrary standards of conduct and rendered im-

---

[11] Cf. Herder's *Ideen* and Schiller's philosophic essays. Cf. p. 132.
[12] Keller designated characters or people he admired in these terms. Cf. p. 55.
[13] XIX, 51, *Der Grüne Heinrich IV*.

possible a correct understanding of inner necessity and human destiny. The most dangerous dogma was that of the Jesuits; although even this "ungeheuere hohle Blase"[14] was no more than a "stockender Fortschritt," it caused nevertheless in its "Weltverbreitung" a noticeable retardation in human progress.[15] The great problem for the present age was to free the intellect from the danger of dogma. Each individual had to seek to clarify himself of subjective notions:

> Wir müssen das edle Pathos des wahren Hasses zur *Reinigung unserer selbst* gegen das wenden, was im allgemeinen Vorrat unserer Eigenschaften, Neigungen, und Zustände dem Jesuitismus den Stoff und die Werkzeuge liefert. (my italics)

A major cause of evil was man's temporary deviation from a pattern of moral conduct because of his vulnerability to the guileful spiritualism of dogmatic teachings.

Keller's conviction that there was no principle of evil and that misdeeds resulted from a lack of moral discernment is further revealed by the fact that he never attributed moral responsibility to a single wrongdoer, no matter how evil his crime. As an example, one need only recall the thief in *Der Grüne Heinrich* who, in his plan to steal Heinrich's gold,[16] was compared with a dog whose eyes and thoughts went no further than the bone in front of it. Heinrich himself occasioned the death of both Lys and his own mother without being aware of what he was doing.[17]

Pankraz der Schmoller, conceived in the early 1850's and like *Der Grüne Heinrich* largely autobiographical in nature,[18] reveals the same belief that ignorance was the seat of wrong. As a boy Pankraz had been rude to mother and sister, and finally, in a sulk, had run away from home. In the course of a varied life,

---

[14] *Ibid.*, 62.
[15] *Ibid.*, p. 61.
[16] XIX, 303.
[17] Heinrich in the original version eventually realized his "guilt," but this "guilt" reflected less Keller's ethics than the personal remorse he had experienced in 1842 when he had learned of the hardship he had caused his mother. Keller himself said he conceived the original ending, in which Heinrich was unwilling to go on living because of his "guilt," at that time (1842) out of "melancholischer Laune." In the revised version, Heinrich's guilt was removed by Judith "als die personifizierte Natur."
[18] Cf. Ricarda Huch, *Gottfried Keller*, p. 19: "Der Grune Heinrich in seiner ersten Form und die erste von den Saldwyler Novellen, Pankraz der Schmoller, sind noch mehr Schöpfungen eines genialen Dranges, als eines göttlichen Geistes . . ." This is the way in which R. Huch stated that both works reflected the same psychological need for self-expression.

he acquired increasing insight. Finally, during a dramatic sulking match with a hostile lion in which each tried to outsulk the other under a burning, tropical sun, Pankraz realized the subjective pattern of his conduct and the wrong-doing of his youth. He returned home and was good to his kin from then on. However, he found it hard to believe that

> eine freundliche oder herbe Gemütsart, nicht nur unser Schicksal und Glück machen, sondern auch dasjenige der uns Umgebenden und uns zu diesen in ein strenges Schuldverhältnis bringen, *ohne dasz wir wissen, wie es zugegangen,* da wir uns ja unser Gemüt nicht selbst gegeben. (VII, 24) (my italics)

Pankraz had the misfortune to possess a "herbe Gemütsart" which caused him unknowingly to do wrong. Yet, like all men, he was basically good, and once enlightened became kind and good.

Die Drei Gerechten Kammacher, a grimly humorous bit of story-telling, again dealt with the problem of wrong-doing as the result of limited understanding. The three righteous comb-makers were actually shallow, selfish creatures whose formal adherence to conventional standards did not resemble either the "himmlische Gerechtigkeit . . . oder die natürliche Gerechtigkeit des menschlichen Gewissens, sondern jene blutlose Gerechtigkeit, welche aus dem Vaterunser die Bitte gestrichen hat." In his repugnance for this type of self-righteous individual, Keller ridiculed the poor rascals mercilessly, but he took pains nevertheless to show that the comb-makers were not villains who acted from conscious premeditation but weak, unenlightened persons unable to act from inner necessity. They resembled Heinrich in his early, superficial conventionalism and differed from him only in their inability to acquire intellectual freedom for themselves.[19]

Before introducing the main plot, Keller showed that the comb-maker Jobst was unethical because he lacked the insight to act from inner necessity. Jobst had sacrificed everything including his humanity and self-respect to save money enough to become an independent *Meister* in Seldwyla. "Das Unmenschliche an diesem so stillen und friedfertigen Plan" was not the plan itself, however, which was "eben so richtig wie begreiflich" but the fact that it did not arise from inner necessity:

---

[19] They could acquire enlightenment only through education. Cf. p. 102.

"Nichts in seinem Herzen zwang ihn, gerade in Seldwyla zu bleiben . . . ." Had Jobst settled in Seldwyla as the result of a free decision based on a recognition of the fact that a change of residence was necessary, his act would have had merit:

> Wo es mir wohl geht, da ist mein Vaterland! heiszt es sonst, und dieses Sprichwort soll auch unangetastet bleiben für diejenigen, welche auch wirklich eine bessere und *notwendige* Ursache ihres Wohlergehens im neuen Vaterlande aufzuweisen haben, welche in *freiem Entschlusse* in die Welt hinausgegangen, um sich rüstig einen Vorteil zu erringen . . . (VII, 266) (my italics)

But Jobst did not have the freewill to recognize necessity and act according to its dictates:

> Aber er hatte keine freie Wahl und ergriff in seinem öden Sinne die erste zufällige Hoffnungsfaser, die sich ihm bot, um sich daran zu hängen und grosz zu saugen. (VII, 266)

His conduct was compared to the unfree acts of the lower animals:

> Auf alle Punkte der Erde sind solche Gerechte hingestreut, die aus keinem anderen Grunde sich dahin verkrümelten, als weil sie zufällig an ein Saugeröhrchen des guten Auskommens gerieten . . . und *gleichen daher weniger dem freien Menschen*, als jenen niederen Organismen, wunderlichen Tierchen und Pflanzensamen, die durch Luft und Wasser an die zufällige Stätte ihres Gedeihens getragen worden. (VII, 267) (my italics)

Thus, though Keller despised the comb-makers, he showed that they lacked moral freewill to act in a necessary fashion and he did not hold them responsible for their misconduct. They never realized that, as Hauch puts it, their "morality was a mere external formula."[20] All their lives they showed themselves to be diligent and consistent. Only the restricted nature of their outlook directed their effort into channels which led to a tragic end. They greeted this end with shocked surprise. To the last they remained unaware of the unethical nature of their conduct.

Viggi Störteler in *Die Miszbrauchten Liebesbriefe* was another such weak character. Since he represented all that Keller detested in literary personalities, Störteler was distorted into a caricature. Notwithstanding, he was not depicted as consciously wicked, for he actually believed in the inane ideas he attempted to force on his wife, and in the literary talent of the self-centered Katie

---

[20] Edward F. Hauch, *Gottfried Keller as a Democratic Idealist*, p. 79.

Amhag. His unnatural ideas, furthermore, revealed a faulty education rather than a basic corruption of character, since he had acquired his ideas in a self-styled literary club to which he had belonged in the years of his apprenticeship. Unlikable as Keller showed him to be, the author never permitted the fact to be obscured that Störteler was at all times completely unaware of his inhumane attitude toward his wife.

A consideration of the three versions of *Der Schmied seines Glückes* shows that the opportunistic barber, John Cabys, was likewise the prey of ignorance, and belies the statement by Ermatinger that "bei ihm (Cabys) sitzt die Lüge nicht in der Hülle, sondern im Herzen" (*Ermatinger* I, 513). In the first version (early 1860's), the barber returned to his shop and lamented his stupidity in consorting with the comely Frau Litumlei, but he never evinced the least trace of guilt; his attitude indicates ignorance and weakness but not a basically evil nature (VIII, 460). In the second version (late 1860's), Cabys became partially enlightened through his experience and became a "Nagelschmied, der in leidlicher Zufriedenheit so dahin hämmerte" (VIII, 461). In the third and final version (1873), the story was given the following conclusion:

> (Cabys) wurde noch ein wackerer Nagelschmied, der erst in leidlicher, *dann in ganzer Zufriedenheit so dahin hämmerte, als er das Glück einfacher und unverdorbener Arbeit spät kennen lernte,* das ihn wahrhaft aller Sorge enthob *und von seinen schlimmen Leidenschaften reinigte.* Nur in stillen Nächten bedachte er noch sein Schicksal . . . allein auch diese Anwandlungen verloren sich allmählich, je besser die Nägel gerieten, welche er schmiedete. (VIII, 112) (my italics)

All three versions reveal that Cabys had been unaware of the arbitrary nature of his opportunism and had never known the nature of honest toil. And the last two versions show that when necessity opened his eyes he was able to derive satisfaction from moral conduct. The error in Ermatinger's claim that "bei ihm sitzt die Lüge im Herzen" is apparent from his statement regarding the final version:

> Mit dem Reste des Geldes . . . kauft er (Cabys) eine alte Nagelschmiede und wird ein eigentlicher Schmied, *auch darin ein moralischer Lump,* dasz er mit der immer gleichen äuszeren Geschicklichkeit den Pinsel des Barbiers mit dem Schmiedehammer vertauschen kann. (*Ermatinger* I, 514) (my italics)

The view that Cabys remained a "moralischer Lump" is certainly in direct conflict with Keller's general attitude and the conclusion of the story.

Many more of Keller's "mixed" characters acted unethically but none were aware of wrongdoing, and not all of them were weak. For example, the clever and devoted mother of Jukundus, in *Das Verlorene Lachen*, did wrong when with Justine she persuaded her son to give up his independence for security; but blinded by a consuming fear of poverty, she was unaware of the selfish nature of her request.

In *Martin Salander* Keller showed with crystal clarity what he had intimated in *Die Miszbrauchten Liebesbriefe* and elsewhere, that incorrect education was responsible for man's misdeeds. The corrupt Weidelich twins were not villains at heart. They merely had not had the good fortune to have Frau Amrain or Herr Jacques' tutor as their educator. They had been led away from a life of moral conduct through the well-meaning but overambitious efforts of their mother and by the short-sightedness of the *Volk* itself which had appointed them to office. As the *Gemeindemann* said after the financial manipulations of the twins had been exposed:

> Eigentlich müszten mir diejenigen den
> Schaden gut machen, die einen solchen
> Menschen zu ihrem Notar wählten und das
> Recht an sich gerissen haben!
> (Hertz VIII, 296)

The twins were not morally responsible. They did not in their hearts feel guilt or shame. Previous to their exposure as manipulators, they had justified their dealings to themselves with the belief that they would repay the money which they had "borrowed" by such devious means. After their exposure and imprisonment, the letters which they wrote to their suffering and needy wives showed neither repentance nor compassion, but brimmed over with continued egotism. They requested food delicacies, the latest newspapers in order to keep in touch with their political districts, and one even requested pen and paper as he felt his experience worthy of autobiographical treatment.

In another connection also, *Martin Salander* showed that intellectual freedom was the answer to the problem of moral conduct and moral responsibility; well-meaning Martin himself would have become unfaithful to his wife out of what he deemed idealistic motives had not his enlightened son Arnold removed the veil from his eyes.[21]

With even the most wicked of his characters, Keller distinguished, then, between the nature of the deed and the nature of the doer. And whereas it was his opinion that inwardly weak individuals could not always of themselves struggle through to enlightenment and moral action, his outlook nevertheless held hope for even such weak characters. Weakness did not mean inner wickedness. In all men the inner voice, the inner necessity reflected the same good and purposeful nature. Had these weak individuals possessed the intellectual freedom to see the necessity for remaining what they essentially were and for doing what they were cut out to do, they might well have led moral and happy lives. As Keller depicted them, Störteler might well have remained a happy business man, and the Weidelich brothers, contented clerks.

How in Keller's optimistic outlook for the future would these weaker individuals acquire intellectual freedom? Through education. In *Frau Regel Amrain*, Keller showed that learning was itself a law of nature and that in a proper environment children could develop "Freiheitssinn" (open mindedness) as a "Denkungsart." And in the great goodness of nature, the battle to clarity did not have to be fought out by every individual since Keller felt that *Freiheitssinn* was something which was transmitted by heredity. This idea of "angeborene Gedanken" was developed in *Der Grüne Heinrich*, in which Keller stated that a part of mankind already possessed *Freiheitssinn*,[22] and was still present in *Martin Salander*: the daughters inherited Martin's "fixe Ideen."[23] Thus, the stronger would maintain and develop their *Freiheitssinn* and the weaker would learn from the strong.

Keller's belief in the goodness of nature and in the morality of all necessary action made him far more liberal and tolerant than most Swiss moralists. He justified for example the infidelity of Lys to his escort Agnes, as well as the suicide of Sali and Vrenele in *Romeo und Julia auf dem Dorfe,* ending the latter

---
[21] Cf. p. 90.
[22] Cf. p. 78, fn. 50.
[23] *Ibid.*

story with the caustic remark that the newspapers saw in the incident a sign of the growing immorality of the times.

Keller's constant interest in *Natur* and *Freiheit* determined his selection of the worst vice and the greatest virtue. The worst vice was vanity; not innocent self-contentedness, but the vanity which led to constant aberration from the course prescribed by inner necessity, so that the individual became "eine Abirrung von sich selbst"[24]—the vanity which blotted out the possibility of an open mind and an enlightened outlook. The greatest virtue was modesty, since modesty implied inner health and an open mind. Every important hero of Keller's was characterized as modest. Sali and Vrenele in *Romeo und Julia auf dem Dorfe*,[25] Fritz Amrain,[26] the tailor Strapinski,[27] Wilhelm the school teacher in *Die Miszbrauchten Liebesbriefe*,[28] the heroine Küngolt in *Dietegen*,[29] Jukundus in *Das Verlorene Lachen*,[30] the sectarians, the mother Ursula and the daughter Agathchen in the same *Novelle*,[31] Karl in *Das Fähnlein der sieben Aufrechten*,[32] Hermine in the same story,[33] Hans Gyr in *Ursala*,[34] the Landvogt von Greifensee,[35] Eugenie in the legend by that name,[36] Arnold Salander,[37] his mother,[38] the father Weidelich,[39] and so one might continue.

A fitting conclusion to a consideration of Keller's ethics is furnished by the charming *Märchen, Spiegel das Kätzchen*. The essence of the tale is the conflict between Spiegel, the representative of intellectual freedom and necessary moral action, and the Hexenmeister, the advocate of subjectivity. With great good humor, Keller revealed Spiegel's enlightened outlook by showing that Spiegel was a cat of principles who knew his nature and

---

[24] XIX, 194-195, *Der Grüne Heinrich IV*.
[25] VII, 163.
[26] VII, 252.
[27] VIII, 9, 23, 30, 35, 68.
[28] VIII, 170.
[29] VIII, 284.
[30] VIII, 316.
[31] VIII, 410.
[32] Hertz, VI, 319, 331.
[33] *Ibid.*, 328.
[34] *Ibid.*, 337, 365.
[35] *Ibid.*, 158, 211, 215.
[36] *Ibid.*, 349.
[37] *Ibid.*, VIII, 348.
[38] *Ibid.*, 27.
[39] *Ibid.*, 326.

what he should and should not do, who acted accordingly, and who consequently never lost his self-respect or peace of mind. Since Spiegel knew, for example, that a moral but masculine-minded cat had at times a need for romantic diversion, he would return from his roof-top escapades the worse for wear but with a clear conscience:

> Wer sich aber nicht schämte, war Spiegel; als ein Mann von Grundsätzen, der wohl wuszte, was er sich zur wohltätigen Abwechslung erlauben durfte, beschäftige er sich *ganz ruhig* damit, die Glätte seines Pelzes und die unschuldige Munterkeit seines Aussehens wiederherzustellen . . . (VII, 325) (my italics)

When Spiegel's mistress died, his sagacity helped him to survive the crisis:

> Doch seine gute Natur, seine Vernunft und Philosophie gaben ihm bald zu fassen, das Unabänderliche zu tragen . . . (VII, 326)

But hard times were in store for Spiegel, and hunger soon lodged on his door-step. The more hungry, the more attentive Spiegel became, and soon "alle seine moralischen Eigenschaften gingen in dieser Aufmerksamkeit auf." His keen wits became so dulled that he begged for food from the most obvious of cat-abusers.

In this weakened condition he accepted the proposition of the town Hexenmeister to trade his life and precious cat-fat for a period of plenty in which he might have his fill of the greatest of delicacies. For a time Spiegel was content to lead this unnatural existence:

> Aber da nun Spiegel ein so herrliches Leben führte, tun und lassen, essen und trinken konnte, was ihm beliebte, und wenn es ihm einfiel, so gedieh er allerdings zusehends an seinem Leibe, sein Pelz wurde wieder glatt und glänzend und sein Auge munter; aber zugleich nahm er, *da sich seine Geisteskräfte in gleichem Masze wieder ansammelten, bessere Sitten an*; die wilde Gier legte sich, und weil er jetzt eine traurige Erfahrung hinter sich hatte, *so wurde er klüger als zuvor*. Er mäszigte sich in seinen Gelüsten und frasz nicht mehr als ihm zuträglich war, indem er zugleich wieder vernünftigen und tiefsinnigen Betrachtungen nachging *und die Dinge wieder durchschaute*. (VII, 333) (my italics)

With renewed physical well-being, Spiegel regained his intellectual freedom and immediately thereupon, his moral nature. Spiegel's "bessere Sitten" consisted in bringing his principles and his nature back into harmony with one another. He gave up his arbitrary manner of living and went back to his natural practice of catching his food on precarious house-tops, his "rechtmäszigen Jagdgrund." As a result, he remained well-fed but did not fatten beyond normal, much to the Hexenmeister's annoyance.

Spiegel thus saved his own life by recognizing his nature and obeying its law. The Hexenmeister, however, whose very profession was arbitrariness, and who symbolized subjectivity, was not so fortunate in his dealings with the clever Spiegel. Since the Hexenmeister was unable to see the true nature of things, Spiegel led him to believe that a horrible old witch was a romantic young maid. The delicious humor of the closing lines reveals the moral of the story:

> Es war ihm (dem Hexenmeister) nicht die geringste *Freiheit* und Erholung gestattet, er muszte hexen vom Morgen bis Abend, was das Zeug halten wollte, und wenn Spiegel vorüberging und es sah, sagte er freundlich; "Immer fleiszig, fleiszig, Herr Pineisz?" (VII, 375) (my italics)

The Hexenmeister's arbitrary way of life lost him his personal freedom.

Thus the *Märchen* showed in clear, simple terms that Keller's ethical belief was rooted in his faith in natural law and intellectual freedom. Spiegel had been moral only as long as he heeded his inner law. When physical weakness dulled his perspicacity, he lost his moral freedom. Renewed physical well-being and recovery of his enlightened outlook meant renewed intellectual freedom, moral behavior, and personal freedom. Willful subjectivity, on the other hand, brought the Hexenmeister a humorously tragic fate and loss of his personal freedom.[40]

---

[40] Ermatinger discusses this *Novelle* from his usual viewpoint of *sittlich-sinnlich* and considers Spiegel as *sittlich* and the Hexenmeister as *sinnlich*. As in the other *Novellen*, Ermatinger does not bring out the importance of enlightenment: "Und auch hier wieder die gleiche Menschlichkeit gegenüber dem sinnlichen Leben. Der Zauberer wird mit einem bösen Weib bestraft, weil er den Hunger des Katers zu schnödem Gewinn ausbeuten will und das edle Vergnügen des Essens durch leckere Henkermahlzeiten prostituiert" (*Ermatinger* I, 354). The result has been that Ermatinger has failed to show the true importance of the Hexenmeister, who was much more significant, in his opposition to Spiegel, as the symbol of a subjective outlook, such as Keller felt the romanticists or the Jesuits taught, than as the symbol of "des sinnlichen Lebens." Dünnebier came closer to the essence of the *Märchen* by making a distinction between *Schein* und *Wesen*, but he too failed to stress the importance of enlightenment.

B. Aesthetics

Keller's shift after 1849 to epic prose as his literary medium, along with comments in which he evidenced disgust for "das subjektive Geblümsel," have often led to the conclusion that here was evidence of a complete change-over in Keller's *Weltanschauung* from lyrical subjectivity to epic objectivity, or from romanticism to realism. If not to Ludwig Feuerbach, then credit was given to the "sobering influence" of the Kapp love-episode or to the university experience in general.

These claims, though there is some truth in them, require much tempering. For one thing, it should be remembered that Keller went to Heidelberg to study a new medium of art, drama, and had thus given up lyric poetry as the prime medium of expression even before his departure from Zürich in October 1848. And if one peers more closely, it becomes evident that as early as 1843, the beginning of the productive lyrical period, Keller had written in his diary about feeling and subjective writing in a way which would not indicate a very profound conviction that lyric mood represented solely, or even best, the reality of life. On July 12, for example, he entered a passage which indicated a knowledge of the fallibility of the lyrical mood:

> Er war ein edler Gefühlsmensch, sein Leben lang für Ideale kämpfend . . . aber er war weniger praktisch . . . *Grosze Enthusiasten sind auch den gröszten Irrtümern unterworfen;* (*Ermatinger* II, 109) (my italics)

In a comment on the ballads of the classical writers, Keller expressed a greater appreciation for the strict, objective form of the ballad than for the subjective form of lyric poems that merely express personal moods:

> Denn obgleich das Balladendichten in strenger Form aus der Mode gekommen zu sein scheint, so möchte es doch schwerer sein, eine Ballade wie Schiller und Goethe sie gemacht haben, hervorzubringen, als das schönste Gedicht, wo der Dichter nur innere Zustände und Gefühle ausspricht. Denn hier braucht er nicht aus sich herauszugehen und darf nur den Schnabel auftun, um die Melodien herausströmen und überschwellen zu lassen, wie sie wollen, während er dort mit dem Stoff, Kostüm und Sitten arbeiten musz. (*Ermatinger* II, 111)

It is of especial significance that as early as 1843 Keller did not trust his self-observation when he felt himself possessed by powerful emotions such as "Leidenschaft und Kummer."[45] If he could not remain "kalt und parteilos" when observing himself, he did not feel it worth the effort "die Gefühle des Augenblickes zu fixieren."[46] Above all he wanted to be "Herr seiner selbst."[47] The powerful desire for intellectual clarity had already asserted its superiority over the interest in subjective mood.

A poem of 1843 also shows a striking distrust of lyrical mood. In the first part of "Auf dem Berge" the poet succumbed to the mood of a beautiful sunset and felt a deep longing to merge himself with the "All." Then suddenly, his reason reasserted itself and he wrote:

> Lasz, o Dichter, solche Träume!
> Sie vergehen mit dem Wind.
> Du versteigest dich in Räume,
> Die dir nie erreichbar sind.
> All die herrlichen Gefilde
> Dort im goldnen Sonnenlicht
> Sind nur leere Traumgebilde
> Und verwirklichen sich nicht.
> (XIII, 36, *Nachgelassene Gedichte*)

Another fact of interest in this connection is that Keller's most lyrical, most personal poems, the *Nachtzyklus,* were descriptions of wild romantic landscapes, "Ossianische Landschaften," such as he had studied and painted for years while in Munich. It would seem that quite a good deal of conscious artistry was employed in these poems, and that the lyrical experience of intimacy with God in the calm of the night was not as *immediate* as often supposed. Not that the lyrical mood was insincere. Such conscious artistic composition would merely indicate that Keller may have analyzed the mood and recreated it in a manner similar to his later method of epic composition when lyric moods were treated "objectively."

A comment in the diary of 1847 indicates rather clearly that Keller considered at least some of his poetry as "official goods" which were more or less a professional responsibility:

> Ist es . . . mir, armer Teufel, nicht zu gönnen, wenn ich der Ware, *welche ich offiziell verfertige und verkaufe*, im Geheimen selbst ein bischen nasche und konsumiere? (*Ermatinger* II, 157)

---

[45] *Ermatinger* II, 114. Gefühle as used here were about equivalent to ideas or convictions.
[46] *Ibid.*
[47] *Ibid.*

It seems likely that Keller's decision to use a subjective medium reflected to some extent his conviction that poetry best suited the propagandistic needs of the time. At least it is definitely recorded in his diary that he felt the need for a powerful medium *to awaken attention*:

> Endlich habe ich etwas von Anastasius Grün bekommen: "Schutt, Dichtungen." Schüchterne, und furchtsame Bemerkungen, dasz die Zeit der Balladen, niedlichen Romanzen und wenigsagenden Tändeleien in elegantem Stil vorbei sein dürfte, und dasz der Dichter mit tiefen Gedanken, groszer nobler Phantasie und schlagender, überquellender Sprache auftreten musz, mehr als je. Er musz, so glaube ich nun bemerkt zu haben, gleich im Anfang Klänge ertönen lassen, welche sich dem besten schon Vorhandenen vergleichen lassen können, *wenn er Aufmerksamkeit erregen will.* (*Ermatinger* II, 110) (my italics)

If one turns to Keller's comments after 1849, one finds further evidence to indicate that the Heidelberg period did not revolutionize his thought as much as has been believed. In a letter of September 1851 to his friend Wilhelm Baumgartner, Keller stated, in discussing Wagner's plan of a merger of the arts to produce the "Kunst der Zukunft," that the individual arts, *including lyric poetry*, could not be replaced:

> Allein daneben wird immer das entschiedene Bedürfnis individueller Virtuosität im einzelnen bestehen bleiben; *das lyrische Gedicht*, das Staffelbild und alle solche Dinge entsprechen einer bestimmten und vorhandenen Gemütslage und Fähigkeit. (*Ermatinger* II, 279) (my italics)

In 1857, though it was his belief that "das jugendliche Bedürfnis häufiger momentaner Stimmungsergüsse ist halt vorbei," Keller still felt a desire to write lyric poetry:

> Ich bin durch die leidige Buchschriftstellerei, die ich handwerklich nicht beherrsche, aus aller Lyrik herausgekommen . . . Seit ich wieder in meiner Heimat bin, spekuliere ich darauf (eine erneute reifere und künstlerische Periode), da ich eigentlich etwas unzweifelhaft Gutes in Liedersachen erst noch zu leisten habe, wenigstens in einem charakteristischen Ensemble. (*Ermatinger* II, 442)

All these facts indicate that the "break" between Keller's "lyric subjectivity" and "epic objectivity" did not involve the complete realignment of thought some scholars seem to think.

The meditations and reflections on the nature of art which

influenced Keller in his mature writings, and which may perhaps best be termed his aesthetics, were carried on during the years 1849-1855 in Heidelberg and Berlin in connection with his preparation to become a dramatist. They dealt primarily with the drama, and were contained in his letters of the period, the Gotthelf essays, and the novel, *Der Grüne Heinrich*.[48] They centered in the idea of *Uebersichtlichkeit*, achieved through uttermost simplicity and clarity. In his terminology and his emphasis on mortality, Keller showed an indebtedness to Feuerbach, but the reader will be left to judge for himself to what extent the basic concepts as developed before 1849 influenced Keller's reasoning.

In a letter of 1851, Keller stated that the writer had to deal solely with nature "ohne Neben- und Hintergedanken":

> Nur für die Kunst und Poesie ist von nun an kein Heil mehr ohne vollkommene geistige Freiheit und ganzes glühendes Erfassen der Natur, ohne alle Neben- und Hintergedanken . . . . (*Ermatinger* II, 275)

The epic writer especially had to represent tangible nature with complete objectivity:

> Zu den äuszern Kennzeichen des wahren Epos gehört, dasz wir alles Sinnliche, Sicht- und Greifbare in vollkommen gesättigter Empfindung mitgenieszen, ohne zwischen der registrirten Schilderung und der Geschichte hin- und hergeschoben zu werden, d.h. dasz die Erscheinung und das Geschehende ineinander aufgehen.[49]

Such objective representation of the visible and tangible in nature did not, however, mean the exclusion of the idea in art. Since Keller was convinced that a great harmony of natural laws pervaded tangible nature, he felt that the true aim of art was to show "das Notwendige" and that all things led back to one "Lebensgrund":

---

[48] Ideas for the art of the future were contained in the essay *Am Mythenstein* (1860). (*Nachgelassene Schriften und Dichtungen*, 5th ed., Berlin: 1893. Verlag von W. Hertz, pp. 53-69.)

[49] Article on J. Gotthelf in *Nachgelassene Schriften und Dichtungen* ed. by J. Baechthold p. 159. The article was written in 1855.

> Denn wie es mir scheint, geht alles richtige Bestreben auf Vereinfachung, Zurückführung und Vereinigung des scheinbar Getrennten und Verschiedenen auf einen Lebensgrund, und in diesem Bestreben *das Notwendige und Einfache mit Kraft und Fülle und in seinem ganzen Wesen darzustellen ist Kunst.*[50]

Actually, then, the purposefulness in nature was to be the subject of art, and the demand for objectivity merely meant that the idea was not to be projected into but drawn from the subject matter. The same held true for motifs. An azure blue, for example, was to be used only where it naturally belonged, as only there it had its real effect:

> Aber sie (azure blue) war hier an ihrem *rechten und gesetzmässigen Platze* und machte daher eine zehnmal poetischere Wirkung als wenn sie in einer erfundenen Landschaft unter anderen Umständen angebracht worden wäre. (XVIII, 23, *Der Grüne Heinrich III*) (my italics)

Thus, *Natur*, both as the manifold of tangible objects and as the great harmony of natural law was to be the subject matter of art.

Keller's ideas on how the writer was to create reflected the influence of both basic concepts. The quotation from the letter of 1851, stating that the artist had to be enlightened and had to depict nature, went on to say that henceforth the artist had also to consider himself "aussschlieszlich sterblicher Mensch"—an obvious tribute to the influence of Feuerbach, but even more, a clear expression and application of Keller's earlier conviction that man was arrayed in the order of nature. A cog in the great wheel of destiny, the artist had to create from inner necessity and his procedure had to resemble "das notwendige und gesetzliche Wachstum der Dinge":

> Das herausspinnen einer fingierten, künstlichen, allegorischen Welt aus der Erfindungskraft, mit Umgehung der guten Natur, ist eben nichts anderes als jene Arbeitsscheu; und wenn Romantiker und Allegoristen aller Art den ganzen Tag schreiben, dichten, malen und operieren, so ist dies alles nur Trägheit gegenüber derjenigen Tätigkeit, *welches nichts anderes ist als das notwendige und gesetzliche Wachstum der Dinge.* Alles Schaffen aus dem Notwendigen und Wirklichen heraus ist Leben und Mühe, die sich selbst verzehren, wie im Blühen das Vergehen schon herannaht. (XVIII, 136, *Der Grüne Heinrich*) (my italics)

---

[50]. XVIII, 8. This principle was expressed by Heinrich *after* reading Goethe, i.e., when he was mature. It is also considered by J. Klinkhammer (*Gottfried Kellers Kunstanschauung*) as expressing the author's opinion.

The degree to which the artist followed this pattern determined the value of his art. Keller considered Gotthelf a great literary genius, despite the lack of polish in his writings, because he felt Gotthelf created from inner necessity:

> Denn nichts Geringeres haben wir daran, als einen reichen und tiefen Schacht nationalen, volksmäszigen, poetischen Ur- und Grundstoffs, *wie er dem Menschengeschlechte angeboren und nicht angeschustert ist* . . .[51] (my italics)

Schiller's life and works were rated highly because he had always created from inner necessity and had done "was er nicht lassen konnte" (XIX, 80):

> Sein Leben ward nichts anderes als die Erfüllung und krystallreine Arbeit der Wahrheit und des Idealen, die in ihm und seiner Zeit lagen. (XIX, 81, *Der Grüne Heinrich IV*)

In the drama, the way in which the writer could be sure to create from inner necessity was to dispense with theatrical effects and to reveal dramatic climaxes long beforehand, so that the audience could experience the full force of the development. He had to strive for "eine vollkommene Uebersicht des Zuschauers":

> Es kommt im Theater lediglich darauf an, an, dasz man komisch oder tragisch erschüttert werde, und das geschieht weit mehr, als durch Ueberraschungen und künstliche Verwicklungen, *durch die vollständige Uebersicht des Zuschauers über die Verhältnisse und Personen.*
> Es sind dieses die edelsten und reinsten, die einzig dramatischen Erschütterungen, welche stufenweise vorher schon empfunden und vorausgesehen worden sind, und wer nach i h n e n trachtet *wird unfehlbar auf der Bahn innerer Notwendigkeit wandeln.* (*Ermatinger* II, 256, Letter to Hettner, 1850) (my italics)

Simplicity and clarity were essential in order to attain the greatest *Uebersicht* possible:

> Damit . . . so viele als immer möglich, damit das g a n z e V o l k auf diesen hohen Standpunkt (der vollständigen Uebersicht), zu diesem wahren Genusse gebracht werden könne, ist auch von selbst die grösztmögliche Einfachheit, Ruhe und Klarheit bedungen . . . (*Ermatinger* II, 257)

Simplicity and clarity as a means to achieve *Uebersicht* were not

---
[51] Cf. fn. 49, p. 109.

only still present in Keller's thoughts a year later (1851), but had become the basic principle of his aesthetics:

> Inzwischen habe ich mir die gröszte Einfachheit und Klarheit zum Prinzip gemacht; keine Intrige und Verwicklung, kein Zufall usw., sondern das reine Aufeinanderwirken menschlicher Leidenschaften und innerlich notwendiger Konflikte; *dabei möglich vollkommene Uebersicht und Voraussicht des Zuschauers* alles dessen, was kommt und wie es kommt; denn nur hierin besteht ein wahrer und edler Genusz für ihn. (*Ermatinger* II, 280) (my italics)

Uebersicht was acclaimed in *Der Grüne Heinrich* (1850-55). Heinrich enjoyed the Tell festival because "man es nicht auf Ueberraschung absah, sondern sich frei herum bewegte und wie aus der Wirklichkeit heraus."[52]

Reducing these statements to their essence, it becomes apparent that Keller strove for simplicity and clarity to achieve the greater clarity or *Uebersicht* which enabled the reader or onlooker to see the action as a whole and feel its necessity. *Uebersicht* may rightly be termed the key to his aesthetic theory.

Though Keller devised the idea of *Uebersichtlichkeit* primarily for the drama, his stories reveal that it was also the principle underlying their structure.[53] *Uebersicht* was attained in a number of ways. It was achieved in part by the use of leading sentences. Thus, in *Der Grüne Heinrich* it was early revealed that the folly of the youth would cost the life of his mother.[54] The forthcoming tragedy of Anna's death was not only foreboded by symbols but also by the direct words of Frau Lee: "sie glaube nicht, dasz das feine, zarte Wesen lange leben würde."[55]

In *Pankraz der Schmoller*, the hero began the story of his love affair with Lydia by revealing his ultimate disillusionment:

> Das heiszt, ich sage: es schien so, oder eigentlich, weisz Gott, ob es am Ende doch so war und es nur an mir lag, dasz es ein solcher *trügerischer* Schein . . . (VII, 39) (my italics)

In *Romeo und Julia auf dem Dorfe*, two such sentences were present. The first revealed the catastrophe of the parents:

---

[52] XVII, 239.

[53] *Uebersichtlichkeit*, it must be clearly understood, was a principle of composition and referred to the development of the action, not to the subtle implications of ideology which might also be present.

[54] XVI, 28.

[55] XVIII, 30.

AESTHETICS

Von diesem Tage an lagen die zwei Bauern im Prozesz mit einander und ruhten nicht, ehe sie beide zugrunde gerichtet waren. (VII, 102)

The second revealed the tragedy of the children:

Denn die armen Leutchen muszten an diesem einen Tage, der ihnen vergönnt war, alle Manieren und Stimmungen der Liebe durchleben und sowohl die verlorenen Tage der zarteren Zeit nachholen als das leidenschaftliche Ende vorausnehmen, mit der Hingabe ihres Lebens. (VII, 162)

Even in *Martin Salander* such a leading sentence was present, though veiled. The washerwoman, Frau Weidelich

wüszte nicht warum sie nicht ebenso gut weisze Bänder tragen dürfte, wie diese und jene, und wenn sie auch keine Rätin sei, so werde sie dereinst vielleicht eines oder zwei solcher Stücke zu Schwiegertöchtern bekommen! (*Hertz* VIII, 8)

Uebersicht was also attained by the use of symbolical episodes, such as the tale of Meretlein in *Der Grüne Heinrich* (the Zwiehan story was substituted in the revised version), which revealed in symbolical fashion the future destiny of Heinrich. Symbolism in a more general sense, plastic representation of an idea or attitude, was the very essence of Keller's style. On the one hand it met the need for dealing with tangible nature; on the other, it allowed for a representation of the attitude which saw "überall nur das Eine und Alles was in allen Dingen wirkt und treibt." At the same time, symbolism was a superb means to heighten *Uebersicht,* since it conduced to simplicity and clarity; a sentiment which Keller voiced when he discussed the symbolical use of action in *Trunk der Vergessenheit*:

Nicht nur wird dadurch die Entwicklung aus dem Gebiete des rhetorischen Räsonnements und der modernen Konversation in eine höhere Region, der poetischen S y m b o l i k, der p l a s t i s c h e n Tat gehoben, welche auszerdem der sinnlichen Natur des Volkes trefflich entspricht; sondern erst durch dieses vorsätzliche Trinken des Fläschchens wird die Sache zu einer *konzentrierten Tat* . . . Erst jetzt durch dieses gewaltsame Handanlegen . . . wird die Schuld . . . plötzlich festgestellt. Erst durch diese frevelhafte Tat wird auch der Wahnsinn *anschaulicher* . . . So wäre die Einheit der Idee gerettet . . . Ich mache Sie noch einmal darauf aufmerksam, wie das Stück erst durch den Trank an eigentlicher Plastik gewinnt . . . *Wir werden auf unserer Bahn der Reinigung und Vereinfachung fortschreiten* . . . (*Ermatinger* II, 260) (my italics)

Keller's frequent recourse to symbolism in all of his prose works is recognized by scholars. Perhaps the most poetic discussion of his symbolism in connection with his *Kunst-* and *Weltanschauung* was contained in the few pages Hugo von Hofmannsthal wrote concerning the little two-room house in *Das Verlorene Lachen,* which in its lighted portion contained the devout sectarians and in its darkened half hid the unsightly *Oelweib.*[56]

Keller further achieved *Uebersicht* by simplifying his vocabulary and style. Rather than employ countless adjectives reflecting every shade of feeling, he restricted himself to a few common adjectives with strong emotional force. The most used pair was "schön" and "unschön" (or "nicht schön"). With nouns the most common pair was "Glück" and "Unglück." In this way Keller taxed the reproductive imagination least and stimulated the creative imagination most, in keeping with his expressed desire for "einfache und starke Empfindungen."[57] Keller, however, in no wise surrendered his artistry for simplicity. Priscilla Kramer in her study of the *Sinngedicht* came to the conclusion that Keller employed a "cyclical method of verbal expression" which she describes as follows:

> Reduced to its lowest terms, this (cyclical) habit manifests itself in the author's apparent reluctance to abandon a stimulating word or thought until all its possibilities have been brought out. To this end, a word may be literally revolved in a paragraph, a page, or even a whole story. It can be shown that this is the technique not only of the *Sinngedicht, but of all Keller's works;* (Op. cit., p. 236) (my italics)

Priscilla Kramer devoted sixty-nine pages of her study to a demonstration of how Keller reiterated a word or idea through "Recurrence, Variation, and Amplification." In this fashion, Keller heightened the artistic effect and increased the clarity, the *Uebersicht,* in his works.

As Keller grew older, the basic concepts came to color his aesthetic views more and more, and the earlier insistence that art develop organically from inner necessity became almost an obsession. Now his own development had always to mirror a

---

[56] Hugo von Hofmannsthal: "Ueber die Schriften von Gottfried Keller," *Die prosaischen Schriften gesammelt,* II, p. 29. For a detailed consideration of Keller's symbolism refer to the study of Paul Settel, *Das Symbolische bei Gottfried Keller,* (typewritten 264 pages), Köln diss., 1921. Extract in *Kölner Jahresbuch* (1921), pp. 40-49.

[57] *Ermatinger* II, 257.

steady progress such as might be found in nature.[58] His style had always to reflect the inner urge; he would say: "Mein Stil liegt in meinem persönlichen Wesen."[59] Words and phrases had to come "fast unbemerkt, wie Früchte vom Baume fallen," and dislike was expressed for "unorganische . . . Wortbildungen."[60] In a plan for a late *Novelle* which was never completed, the desire for organic motifs was apparent:

> Der Untergang des Starken geht einer geplanten schlechten Tat voran, so dasz er *organisch* zur Peripetie oder Entwicklung zum Guten notwendig wird. (*Ermatinger* I, 609) (my italics)

But at the same time he still maintained that the author had to remain master of his material and as late as 1884 criticized the naturalistic writer Hermann Friedrichs for his lack of detachment and perspective:

> Was mir bei aller Korrektheit ihrer Arbeit mangelt, ist eine gewisse gute Laune, ein gewisser Sonnenschein, *eine Freiheit des Geistes*, die über der Schrift schweben und derselben den Charakter des fleiszig gelösten Pensums, der bloszen Mache benehmen. (*Ermatinger* I, 541) (my italics)

The writer had to maintain his freedom.

Freiheit as the ultimate goal of humanity also caused Keller to believe that the art of the future would require new forms. Writing to his friend Hettner, in 1851, he urged him not to discard the historical trilogy as a poetic medium, as the day would come when the *Volk* would be "gebildet und bewuszt" and a trilogy could be employed.[61] Keller's belief in human progress to enlightenment also influenced his grandiose vision of a national choir and huge national dramatic festivals in which the entire *Volk* would participate.[62]

The importance of *Natur* and *Freiheit* to Keller's aesthetics is obvious. *Natur* in both its aspects was the subject of art. The purpose of art was to show the one *Lebensgrund* of all things and (in drama) to create the illusion of necessary development by means of *Uebersicht*. The artist had to be enlightened and create from inner necessity. The art of the future would have to be adapted to meet the needs of the enlightened *Volk*.

---

[58] Letter of the 1860's to Julius Rodenberg.
[59] *Ermatinger* III, 133. Letter to Emil Kuh, 1882.
[60] *Ibid.*, 488. Letter to J. W. Widmann, 1885.
[61] *Ermatinger* II, 285.
[62] *Am Mythenstein*, pp. 53-69. Cf. fn. 48.

C. *Politics*

Keller's nature-idealism led him to conceive of the *Volk* as a dynamic entity with an organic life-cycle and an inner purpose of its own. A people was born, waxed until maturity (*Blütezeit*) when its latent potentialities were brought to expression, and then sank back into oblivion. The life-span of a people depended on the time needed to carry out its mission, to bring its inner germ to fruition. The more enlightened a people was, the more it realized its inner necessity and the better it could fulfill its destiny.

This notion of the *Volk* was already implicit in Keller's early lyrics of freedom in such lines as "Wenn aus der Völker Schwellen und Versanden ein Neues sich zum Ganzen einreiht";[63] it was clearly expressed in *Der Grüne Heinrich*[64] and in two political stories, *Das Fähnlein der sieben Aufrechten* (1860)[65] and *Martin Salander* (1886).[66] To be sure, in the twenty-six years which separated the latter works, Keller changed from a liberal to a conservative in Swiss politics, but this shift did not imply a change in his fundamental outlook; it did not alter his conception of the *Volk*. In *Das Fähnlein*, the hero Karl felt that an enlightened people could best realize its destiny by unceasing activity:

> Ein Volk, welches weisz, dasz es einst nicht mehr sein wird, nützt seine Tage um so lebendiger, lebt um so länger und hinterläszt ein rühmliches Gedächtnis; denn es wird sich keine Ruhe gönnen, bis es die Fähigkeiten, die in ihm liegen, ans Licht und zur Geltung gebracht hat, gleich einem rastlosen Manne, der sein Haus bestelle, ehe denn er dahin scheidet. Dies ist nach meiner Meinung die Hauptsache! (*Hertz* VI, 277)

In *Martin Salander*, Arnold, the advocate of enlightenment who was aware of the "Bedingungswerte der Geschichte,"[67] still believed that a *Volk* had to follow its inner destiny, and consequently, that the freedom, which was the ultimate goal of the people, should not be reached prematurely through the adoption of a rationally conceived, democratic constitution:

---

[63] XIV, 76, *Nachgelassene Gedichte*, "Vaterländische Sonette" No. 10.
[64] XIX, 60.
[65] *Hertz* VI, 27.
[66] *Hertz* VIII, 160.
[67] Cf. p. 89 in this study.

> Es sei ein Naturgesetz, dasz alles Leben, je rastloser es gelebt werde, um so schneller sich auslebe und ein Ende nähme; daher ... vermöge er es nicht gerade als ein zweckmäsziges Mittel zur Lebensverlängerung anzusehen, wenn ein Volk *die letzte Konsequenz, deren Keim in ihm stecke,* vor der Zeit zu Tode hetze und damit sich selbst. (*Hertz* VIII, 160) (my italics)

Keller objected to the new democratic constitution because it did not reflect the latent "wahre Verfassung" which existed within the people itself:

> Eine Verfassung ist aber keine stilistische Examenarbeit. Die sogenannten logischen, schönen, philosophischen Verfassungen haben sich nie eines langen Lebens erfreut. Wäre mit solchen geholfen, so würden die überlebten Republiken noch da sein, welche sich einst bei Rousseau Verfassungen bestellten, *weil sie kein Volk hatten, in welchem die wahren Verfassungen latent sind bis zum letzten Augenblick.* Uns scheinen jene Verfassungen die schönsten zu sein, in welchen, ohne Rücksicht auf Stil und Symmetrie, ein Konkretum, ein errungenes Recht neben dem andern liegt, wie die harten glänzenden Körner im Granit, und welche zugleich, die klarste Geschichte ihrer selbst sind. (*Ermatinger* I, 421) (my italics)

The corruption which Keller attacked so bitterly did not cause a change in his basic belief in the goodness of natural law. He still felt that such periods of moral confusion were part of a great rhythm and represented nothing more than "stockender Fortschritt":[68]

> Die Korruption, der sittliche Verfall des Volksstaates ist so gut der Regeneration fähig wie das Körperliche des Volkes, durch Reaktion seiner Kräfte, natürliche Polizei, Ausruhen; *es ist ja überall in der Geschichte dieser Rhythmus vom Sinken und Erheben.* Glücklich, wenn die Perioden nur so lange dauern, dasz die Erinnerung an das Glück derjenigen an das Uebel das Gleichgewicht hält. (Baechthold's biography, III, 645, "Materialien") (my italics)

The inner unity of a people was not founded on racial similarity but on a common historical mission, a common inner necessity. Not physical resemblance, but "Lieb und Bedürfnis"[69] were what went to make a new people. The basic unifying force was "Gleichgesinnung."[70] In 1841 Keller had felt that a "vorsätz-

---
[68] Cf. pp. 61-62, 97 in this study.
[69] XIV, 76, *Nachgelassene Gedichte*, "Vaterländische Sonette" No. 10.
[70] *Ibid.*

liche Nichtbeachtung unseres Nationalcharakters" had led to a misunderstanding of the inner unity of the Swiss:

> Denn zugegeben, dasz wir den nämlichen Völkerstämmen entsprossen sind wie unsere Nachbarn, so tut das durchaus nichts zur Sache. Der Geist der Generationen verändert sich unendlich und wenn wir jener Ansicht und der Bibel folgen müszten, so wäre die ganze Menschheit nur e i n e Nation und müszte folglich nur einen einzigen Staat ausmachen. Die jetzige Bevölkerung Englands ist entstanden aus Britanniern, Römern, Angelsachsen, Normannen, Kelten usf., die alle einander wechselweise besiegt, verdrängt, und unterdrückt haben, und doch ist die englische Nation jetzt eine ganze, unteilbare, originell in ihrem Charakter und weder den jetzigen Franzosen noch Deutschen noch irgendeinem Volke ähnlich. So ist's auch mit den Schweizern gegangen.[71]

This statement may of course be interpreted merely as the expression of Keller's patriotic feeling, but it is in perfect accord with his broader idealism.

As Keller's cosmic outlook included all men, he did not consider the *Volk* to be an end in itself, but a segment of mankind destined to carry out a special task.[72] Thus, when a people had fulfilled its mission and its end was near, there was no cause for regret or mourning. Even with regard to his beloved Switzerland, Keller saw no reason for a nostalgic procrastination of the final day:

> Ist die Aufgabe eines Volkes gelöst, so kommt es auf einige Tage längerer oder kürzerer Dauer nicht mehr an, *neue Erscheinungen harren schon an der Pforte ihrer Zeit!* (*Hertz* VI, 277) (my italics)

The important thing was that the progress toward universal intellectual freedom went on unimpeded. Heinrich realized that there was no cause for remorse since the contributions of past peoples lived on in the present and continued to serve mankind in its march toward universal enlightenment:

> Heinrich trug ein zwiefaches praktisches Ergebnis von seinem Selbstunterricht in der Geschichte davon. Erstlich gewöhnte er sich gänzlich ab, irgend einen entschwundenen Völkerzustand, und sei er noch so glänzend gewesen, zu beklagen, da dessen Untergang der erste Beweis seiner Unvollständigkeit ist. Er be-

---

[71] H. M. Kriesi, *op. cit.*, 244, *Anhang.* Cf. also Jonas Fränkel, *Gottfried Kellers Politische Sendung*, pp. 18-19. (Fränkel's work sought to refute alleged German propaganda in the form of studies on Keller. It discusses in detail Keller's differentiation between *Volk und Rasse.*)

[72] Note the similarity to Herder's *Ideen.*

dauerte nun weder die beste Zeit des Griechentums noch des Römertums, da das, was an ihr gut und schön war nichts weniger als vergangen, sondern in jedes bewuszten Mannes Bewusztsein lebendig ist und in dem Grade, nebst anderen guten Dingen, *endlich wieder hervortreten wird als das Bewusztsein der Menschengeschichte, d.h. die wahre menschliche Bildung allgemein werden wird.* (XIX, 60, *Der Grüne Heinrich IV*) (my italics)

Heinrich felt that though peoples died out, the flesh did not, so that, in accordance with his belief (and Keller's) in "angeborene Gedanken" and in the inheritability of virtues and attitudes, some modern people were of the same flesh and blood as the Greeks and Romans and possessed their virtues:

Insofern bestimmte Geschlechter und Personen die Träger der Tugenden vergangener Glanztage sind, müssen wir ihnen, *da diese Hingegangenen Fleisch von unserem Fleische sind,* den Zoll weihen, der allem Wesentlichen, was war und ist gebührt ... (XIX, 61, *Der Grüne Heinrich IV*) (my italics)

The final human product was not *völkisch* but *menschlich*. Ultimately, man was to become a "besonnener, freier Staats- und Weltbürger" who possessed the "ruhigen festen Gleichmut" that came from an awareness of the moral law in history and with full enlightenment:

Der ruhige, feste Gleichmut, *welcher aus solcher Auffassung des Ganzen und Vergleichung des Einzelnen* (in der Geschichte) hervorgeht, glücklich gemischt mit lebendigem Gefühl und Feuer für das nächst zu Ergreifende und Selbsterlebte, macht erst den guten und wohlgebildeten Weltbürger aus. (XIX, 68) (my italics)

The final form of government was to be a republic of the world governed by the one immutable law of all things, the moral law. In *Das Verlorene Lachen* Jukundus had expressed the belief that one day this would come to pass.[73] Keller's political ideal was symbolically shown in his description in *Der Grüne Heinrich* of a small Swiss town in which there was both personal freedom and immutable laws:

Es herrschte jene Verschiedenheit und Individualität, wie sie durch die unbeschränkte persönliche Freiheit erzeugt wird, jene Freiheit, welche bei einer unerschütterlichen Strenge der Gesetze, jedem sein Schicksal überläszt und ihn zum Schmied seines eigenen Glückes macht. (XVI, 31)

---

[73] Cf. p. 78 in this study.

However, Keller realized that such a republic could not be achieved on earth before intellectual freedom became universal. Jukundus had associated his republic with the time when "Alle um Alles wüszten." Until such a time Keller felt that rulers would mislead their peoples with regard to the true nature of government:

> Angesichts dieser Tatsache wird wohl nur darum die Republik in der weiten Welt fast unmöglich, weil sie von ihren Verkündigern anstatt zur Sache der kühlen Vernunft und Lebenspraxis, zur Sache des Gefühls, zum religiösen Ideal gemacht wird, welches wieder der Heuchelei, der Schwärmerei und einem politischen Pfaffentum Tür und Tor öffnet. (XVI, 53, *Der Grüne Heinrich I*)

Thus the idealism implicit in *Natur* and *Freiheit* also colored Keller's political views, making him devoted to his *Volk* but dedicated to a cause which included all humanity—intellectual freedom.

D. *Social Relations*

Until his later years, when he became politically conservative, Keller was progressive in his views on human relations and on institutions which objectivized these relations. This attitude was born of the conviction that all human activity was inspired by the inner moral spark, the moral law, and that all outward expression and concretion of that inner force were as yet relative and finite. Since life was a constant change and an onward march toward ultimate universal "menschliche Bildung,"[74] Keller never looked at institutions as venerable edifices of the past to be preserved and cherished for all time, but as manifestations of the moral law, as concretions of the expression of human need, as entities which were subjective, relative, alterable, and finite. The complicated legal code known as Roman law, for example, was viewed not as an entity unto itself but as something which had developed from man's *Rechtsgefühl*. The present system of abstract principles had grown out of simpler, concrete forms, which in turn were the expression of man's sense of justice (his moral sense):

> Er (der Grüne Heinrich) sah aus den naturwüchsig konkreten Anfängen mit ihren plastischen Gebräuchen das allgemeinste in

---

[74] Cf. p. 119 in this study.

sich selbst ruhende Rechtsleben hervorgehen, zu einer ungeheueren
für Jahrtausende maszgebenden Disziplin sich entwickeln, doch in
jeder Faser eine Abspiegelung der Menschenverhältnisse, ihrer
Bestimmungen, Bedürfnisse, Leidenschaften, Sitten und Zustände,
Fähigkeiten und Mängel, Tugenden und Laster darstellen. Er
sah wie dieses ganze Wesen, dem Rechts- und Freiheitsgefühl
einer Rasse entsprossen . . . (XIX, 58)

Roman Law was to be preferred to German law, despite the later's hoary venerability and romantic tradition, because Roman Law was better designed to further "Recht und Freiheit":

. . . (Roman law) war eher geeignet, unter den betrübtesten Verhältnissen den Sinn des Rechtes und mit diesem den Sinn der Freiheit, wenn auch schlafend, aufzubewahren, als das germanische Recht, welches seiner Gewohnheitsnatur, seiner eigensinnigen Liebhabereien, seines äuszerlichen Gebrauchswesens und seines unechten Individualismus halber sich unfähig gezeigt hat, den vielgerühmten germanischen Sinn für Recht und Freiheit im ganzen und groszen zu erhalten, so wenig als sich selbst. (XIX, 58)

Government, state and *Volk* were all relative quantities, finite and subject to change. The coup d'état of 1847 was justified by Keller as a natural and organic part of the development of the confederation:

Das Land war mitten in dem Kampfe und in der Mauser begriffen, welche mit dem Umwandlungsprozesse eines Jahrhunderte alten Staatenbundes in einen Bundesstaat abschlosz *und ein durchaus denkwürdiger, in sich selbst bedingter, organischer Prozesz war* . . . (XIX, 310, *Der Grüne Heinrich IV*) (my italics)

His later political conservatism reflected no actual change in basic attitude. He objected to the democratic constitution of 1869 on the ground that it did not evolve from the spirit of the *Volk* itself or from Swiss tradition, but was foisted on the nation from without, and he was convinced that only acts or institutions which possessed inner necessity could stand the test of time. Though an advocate of democracy, he felt democracy had come to Switzerland prematurely. Keller considered his beloved Swiss *Volk* not as an end in itself but merely as an organic unit conceived by nature to facilitate the general human development toward enlightenment and moral freedom. The *Volk* was finite—finite in Keller's outlook even before 1849[75]—and when its task

---

[75] Cf. quotation at bottom of p. 25 in this study.

was done no regret was to be felt for its passing.[76] The *Volk* was to be loved and cherished, yes, but as a part of, not as superior to, the rest of humanity. It was the dynamic element in Keller's *Weltanschauung* that lifted him above the narrow ideals of state patriotism to loftier humanitarian goals.

Nor did Keller view religion in terms of the orthodox confessions, but rather in terms of its source in human feeling and experience. Religion arose from man's basic "Gefühl unschuldiger und naiver Zufriedenheit, welches alle Menschen umfängt, wenn sie gern und leicht an das Gute, Schöne und Merkwürdige glauben . . ." (XVI, 205), and to understand religion one had to observe living faith in sectists and primitive people:

> Will man die Bedeutung des Glaubens kennen, so musz man nicht sowohl die orthodoxen Kirchenleute betrachten, bei denen der Institutionen wegen alles über einen Kamm geschoren ist und das Eigentümliche daher zurücktritt, als vielmehr die undisziplinierten Wildlinge des Glaubens, welche auszerhalb der Kirchenmauern frei umherschwirren, sei es in entstehenden Sekten, sei es in einzelnen Personen. Hier treten die rechten Beweggründe und das Ursprüngliche in Schicksal und Charakter hervor *und werfen Licht in das verwachsene und fest gewordene Gebilde der groszen geschichtlichen Masse.* (XVI, 206, *Der Grüne Heinrich I*) (my italics)

Keller himself had early in life broken with traditional religious beliefs as outmoded and, after hearing Feuerbach, had dispensed with the conventional Christian God entirely. Thus, Keller viewed the great religious institutions sociologically as relative and finite entities filling a spiritual need of the people of their time, but eventually to be superseded by universal religious freedom.

The status quo of the economic system was nothing to be preserved. Keller was not loath to see the agricultural economy yield to the new industrial era and insisted in an early and now famous poem that industrialization would not end the charm of the countryside and poetic motifs, rather that it would furnish new sources of poetic feeling such as dirigibles.[77]

Although he always felt greatly his loss at not having had sufficient formal schooling in his youth, Keller seldom dealt with formal institutions and formal curricula in his views on education. His theme, as shown in *Frau Regel Amrain*, was that

---

[76] Cf. p. 118 in this study.
[77] XIV, 253-255.

education should involve a minimum of formality and should impede the natural development of a child as little as possible. Education entailed the development of personality, the guidance necessary to further a child's mental growth to an enlightened, mature outlook, the inculcation of habits of modesty and straightforwardness which enabled acts to reflect inner necessity, and was to be conveyed less by word than by example. Herr Jacques learned from his tutor that the most important thing of all was to act from inner necessity. The goal of education was not formal or objective acquisition of facts, but the development of a mature personality free from preconceptions.

Keller's ideas on the nature of work and the choice of a vocation also reflect the influence of the basic concepts in his thought. True work (*wirkliche Arbeit*) had to possess two attributes—honest effort and inner necessity. "Ein bloszes Wollen, ein glücklicher Einfall" which led to "reichlichen Erwerb,"[78] a shrewd idea such as John Cabys had had, did not represent true work; nor did "eine nachhaltige Mühe ... ohne innere Wahrheit, ohne vernünftigen Zweck, ohne Idee"[79] as represented in Keller's eyes by the comb-makers, who had no real reason for wanting to settle in Seldwyla. When man had been close to the soil, "die Heiligkeit und die Bedeutung der Arbeit" had still been clear to him and he had recognized work to be a "Naturpflicht."[80] But in the complex of modern society, people did their work with varying degrees of sincerity. Keller illustrated what he meant by real and sincere work in a reference to Schiller:

> Will man hingegen aus der groszen öffentlichen Welt ein Beispiel wirkungsreicher Arbeit, die zugleich ein wahres und vernünftiges Leben ist, betrachten, so musz man das Leben und Wirken Schillers ansehen. Dieser ... nur das tuend, was er nicht lassen konnte ... veredelte sich unablässig von innen heraus und sein Leben ward nichts anderes als die Erfüllung seines innersten Wesens, die folgerechte und krystallreine Arbeit der Wahrheit und des Idealen, die in ihm und seiner Zeit lagen .... Aber nach seinem Tode erst, kann man sagen, begann sein ehrliches, klares und wahres Arbeitsleben seine Wirkung und seine Erwerbsfähigkeit zu zeigen ... (XIX, 81)

In this passage it is also apparent how a choice of vocation should be made. One's life should be the "Erfüllung seines innersten

---
[78] XIX, 78.
[79] *Ibid.*
[80] *Ibid.*, 77.

Wesens," and one's life-work, that for which one was naturally suited without regard for the acquisition of fame or riches (*Strebertum*). Not only was such recognition of and obedience to the inner law the moral thing to do, but it was also the only way to achieve happiness. Very few people ever achieved happiness or success by following any other course:

> Gegenüber diesem einheitlichen organischen Leben gibt es nun auch ein gespaltenes, getrenntes, gewissermaszen unorganisches Leben, wie wenn Spinoza und Rousseau grosze Denker sind ihrem innern Berufe nach und, um sich zu ernähren, zugleich Brillengläser schleifen und Noten schreiben. Diese Art beruht auf einer Entsagung, welche in Ausnahmsfällen dem selbstbewuszten Menschen wohl ansteht, als Zeugnis seiner Gewalt. Die Natur selbst aber weist nicht auf ein solches Doppelleben, und wenn diese Entsagung, die Spaltung des Wesens eines Menschens allgemeingültig sein sollte, so würde sie die Welt mit Schmerz und Elend erfüllen. So fest und allgemein wie das Naturgesetz selber sollen wir unser Dasein durch das nähren, was wir sind und bedeuten, und das mit Ehren sein, was uns nährt. Nur dadurch sind wir ganz, bewahren uns vor Einseitigkeit und Ueberspanntheit und leben mit der Welt im Frieden, so wie sie mit uns, indem wir sie sowohl bedürfen mit ihrer ganzen Art, mit ihrem Genusz und ihrer Müh, als sie unser bedarf zu ihrer Vollständigkeit, und alles das, ohne dasz wir einen Augenblick aus unserer wahren Bestimmung und Eigenschaft herausgehen. (XIX, 82, *Der Grüne Heinrich IV*)

However, the correct choice of a vocation called for an enlightened outlook, since without enlightenment man could not interpret inner necessity correctly and be aware of his true "Bestimmung." All men were to some degree the "Meisternaturen, die zweifelsohne jeden Augenblick vorhanden sind, und unbewuszt hinter ihrem Pfluge gehen oder auf dem Dreifusz des Schusters sitzen." But only those men who knew at the right time "in sich zu gehen," to recognize inner necessity and their destiny, were truly happy:

> Im Grunde sind trotz aller äuszeren Schicksale nur die Meister glücklich, d.h. die das Geschäft verstehen, was sie betreiben, *und wohl jedem, der zur rechten Zeit in sich zu gehen weisz.* Er wird, einen Stiefel zurechthämmernd, ein souveräner König sein neben dem hypochondrischen Ritter vom Dilettantismus, der im durchlöcherten Ordensmantel melancholisch einherstolziert. (XIX, 88) (my italics)

Here, as everywhere, *Natur* and *Freiheit* were the basic standards, the basic premises, from which Keller developed the pattern of his thought.

CHAPTER 4

SCHILLER AND KELLER

A consideration of the influence of Schiller's ideas on Keller is here of interest, since it offers interesting sidelights confirming some of the main hypotheses of this study. By showing there is strong reason to believe that Schiller's philosophical essays, especially *Ueber Naive und Sentimentalische Dichtung*, were the source of Keller's conception of freedom,[1] further evidence is supplied to support the contention that Keller did not derive his early ideas from the romantic writers and that his early freedom was not the arbitrary freedom of the romantic ego. By revealing that Keller throughout his life respected and admired Schiller both as a man and as a defender of the inviolable freedom of the spirit, additional arguments are furnished to show that Keller was deeply and constantly interested in inner freedom, and that his *Weltanschauung* was not characterized by change but by a tenacious adherence to early conceptions—a man seldom respects the heroes of his youth if he has drastically altered his outlook. It should be expressly noted that no attempt will be made to prove that Keller and Schiller had similar philosophies, for Keller was a monist and Schiller a dualist.[2] What is contended is that it seems highly probable that Keller derived his basic notions *from his own interpretation* of Schiller's ideas.

All in all, it is not surprising that scholars have never made any serious attempt to trace Keller's early ideas back to Schiller. The reason for this is not to be found in the fact, however, that the former's outlook was monistic and emphasized enlightenment as the means to freedom whereas the latter's was dualistic and emphasized beauty, since few scholars considered Keller's early outlook as other than romantically dualistic.[3] The important reason was rather that, since by his own admission in *Der*

---

[1] A separate discussion of *Natur* will not be undertaken since the concept of natural law was too generally held to allow for a conclusive demonstration of influence, and since the idea of natural law is already implicit in the concept of *Freiheit*.

[2] There is little likelihood that the young Keller understood the Kantian dualism which was the basis of Schiller's thought. The former's ideas seem taken mostly from *Ueber Naive und Sentimentalische Dichtung*, in which natural law and moral law are treated with equal reverence and are placed in the same sphere.

[3] Even Dünnebier considered the nature and freedom referred to in the letter of 1837 to be romantically subjective, *op. cit.*, p. 3.

Grüne Heinrich Keller had been a romanticist in his youth, and since everything "unromantic" in his mature philosophy was ascribed to Feuerbach[4] (in a few instances Goethe for such lines as "so einfach still zu sein wie die Natur"), romantic influences such as Jean Paul and Novalis[5] sufficed to explain his early attitude.

Then also, Keller's early interest in freedom was generally mistaken to pertain primarily to political freedom. This was occasioned by a number of factors. Keller had written many of his early lyrics in the style of the political poets—Grün, Herwegh, and Freiligrath. He had ostensibly been an active member of a political circle which consisted mostly of intellectual revolutionaries, and the leader of the group, August Follen, had been his editor and publisher. He seemed to fit most neatly into the long tradition of *Schweizerfreiheit*, which was political freedom in a republican state. Lastly, the studies which dealt with the content of his early lyrics were made mostly by students of history and political science who were not interested in the philosophical aspects of his use of *Freiheit*.[6]

The possibility of an ideological bond between Keller and Schiller was denied categorically by Müller-Gschwend in a study of Keller's lyrics. Müller-Gschwend felt that Keller's poems were "denen Schillers innerlich fremd" and that "'sein Ideal ist nicht Schönheit sondern hinreiszende Wirkung.'"[7] Though scholars now agree that Keller in his early years was not a mere revolutionary with a political outlook,[8] Müller-Gschwend's conclusions still stand and are beginning to acquire the authority that comes with the passage of time.

---

[4] Cf. discussion of Ermatinger, Dünnebier and others in the appendix.

[5] Cf. Frieda Jaeggi, *Gottfried Keller und Jean Paul*; Paul Meintel, *Gottfried Keller und die Romantik*; Anna Weiman-Bischoff, *Gottfried Keller und die Romantik*. A discussion of these works is furnished in the appendix, pp. 140-142.

[6] Better known studies of this type are: C. F. Hauch, *Gottfried Keller, a democratic idealist*; H. M. Kriesi, *Gottfried Keller als Politiker*; E. Howald, *Gottfried Keller, Schweizer, Deutscher, Dichter, Weltbürger*.

[7] Gustav Müller-Geschwend, *Gottfried Keller als Lyrischer Dichter*, Strassburg diss., 1910, p. 10.

[8] Cf. Max Hochdorf, *Gottfried Keller im europäischen Gedanken*, 1919, p. 12. Hochdorf said with regard to the young Keller's political interest, "Ihm liegt wenig an dem Aufruhr, wenn die Erleuchtung nicht auch in das Gewissen der Menschheit dringt." Fränkel also indicated that many dramatic touches in Keller's early poems were due to Follen's editing (II, xx). In *Der Grüne Heinrich*, Keller depicted himself as the observant outsider rather than as a political activist.

And yet the interesting fact remains that while Keller scholars have never made any serious attempt to correlate the philosophies of Schiller and Keller, almost all of them were nevertheless compelled at one time or another to recognize the bond between the two men. Agnes Waldhausen, for example, granted the fact that Keller had been familiar with Schiller's works long before he had read Goethe,[9] while Hans Dünnebier admitted that Keller stood closer to Schiller than to the Swiss didactic writers.[10] Emil Ermatinger, who insisted that the two men were philosophically worlds apart, conceded that Keller's early dramatic fragments were imitations of Schiller's dramas.[11] Gleichen-Russwurm found it significant that Keller adhered to Schiller's principle of having character determine outer appearance.[12] An earlier critic Eduard Korrodi, had even ventured to state, but merely to state, that with the *Prolog* of 1859 Keller had reached Schiller's *Freiheitsbegriff*.[13]

With this picture of the critical literature by way of introduction, let us now turn to the set of facts which indicate that Keller derived his conception of freedom from Schiller's works.

Keller's concept of *Freiheit* as moral freedom based on enlightenment first appeared in a letter, now recognized by scholars for its philosophic sincerity, which was written when he was only seventeen years old.[14] A consideration of his biography limits the possible sources for the concept to three: the ideas current in the spirit of the times, popular books, and the classics in his father's library.

Although the strong Swiss tradition of political independence could have awakened only indirectly the youth's interest in ethical

---

[9] Agnes Waldhausen, *Euphorion* XVI (1909), pp. 471-497. "Früher als Goethes, hatte Schillers Name einen bedeutenden Klang für Keller gehabt, da er in seines Vaters hinterlassenen Bibliothek Schillers Werke fand."

[10] Hans Dünnebier, *op. cit.*, p. 165. "Mit seiner Ueberzeugung von der sittlichen Kraft und Wirkung der Poesie steht Keller jenem deutschen Dichter, den er immer als Ideal eines Menschen und Künstlers bewundert hat, viel näher als jenen Volkspädagogen (Gotthelf, Hirzel, Pestalozzi), nämlich Schillern."

[11] *Ermatinger* I, 26, 265, 267.

[12] Gleichen-Russwurm: *Gottfried Kellers Weltanschauung*, p. 78. "Oft geht die Parallelerscheinung des Äuszern und Innern soweit, dasz der Körper sich gleichzeitig mit dem Charakter ändert—eine dichterische Deutung von Schillers Gedanken: Es ist der Geist, der sich den Körper baut."

[13] Eduard Korrodi: *Gottfried Keller Ein Deutscher Lyriker*, pp. 94-95. "Erst auf dem Umweg über die Revolutionsdichtung kam Gottfried Keller zu den abgeklärten Freiheitsideen Schillers." "Und just da er Schiller feiert (1859), nähert sich auch seine Freiheitsidee derjenigen des weimarischen Groszen."

[14] *Ermatinger* II, 5. Letter of 1837 to Müller.

freedom, the ebbing Swiss enlightenment, at the time still a factor in the national intellectual environment, might have exerted a more direct influence. It is conceivable that two devotees of the Enlightenment, Johann Heinrich Pestalozzi and Heinrich Zschokke, inspired Keller, as they were still widely read in his youth. Pestalozzi, especially, who through Bodmer stood close to Leibniz, had ideas similar to Keller's. Pestalozzi felt that human wickedness would end with the triumph of the moral freewill. He viewed human development as progress from a state of blind acceptance to a state of voluntary acceptance of nature.[15] Even here, however, the parallelism of ideas is striking only in the broader outlines, and it is far more probable that the profound philosophical implications inherent in Keller's *Freiheit* were acquired from readings in his father's library, where he became acquainted with numerous romantic writers and with the classic exponent of freedom, Friedrich Schiller.

Two factors indicate Schiller's influence. First, Schiller's works formed a major part of the impressionable youth's intellectual environment, and it is an established psychological fact that strong impressions gained in youth tend to be the most lasting. Keller's father admired Schiller and his enthusiasm might well have carried over to his son[16]—if not directly, then through the medium of Keller's mother.[17] From *Der Grüne Heinrich* and the *Autobiography* of 1876, it is clear that Keller had read Schiller's complete works, the jewel of his father's library, before the age of thirteen,[18] and as far as he was able, mastered their contents:

> Mein Trieb mich zu unterrichten und zu unterhalten, und meine Sammlungslust führten mich überall hin, wo alte Bücher, Kupferstiche, und sonstige Dinge zu kaufen waren; denn die Bücher meines Vaters, deren Hauptzierde Schiller war, hatte ich längst, soweit sie mir verständlich, durchgelesen und zu eigen gemacht und selbst das Unverständliche übersetzte ich in eine eigene erfundene fabelhafte Wissenschaft, mit Worten spielend; (XVII, 138)

---

[15] J. H. Pestalozzi: *Meine Nachforschungen über den Gang der Natur in der Entwicklung des Menschengeschlechts.*

[16] XVI, 84-85. In *Der Grüne Heinrich*, Keller gave a detailed account of his father's interest in Schiller and Schiller's dramas.

[17] *Ermatinger* I, 7.

[18] In his autobiography of 1876, Keller stated that a moving story induced him as a thirteen-year-old youth to a dramatization of the story and the "Anfertigung eines ausführlichen Scenariums nach Vorbild der Schillerschen Nachlaszwerke." *Nachgelassene Schriften und Dichtungen,* ed. by Baechthold, p. 15.

In 1834, a large number of dramas, including many by Schiller, were performed in a converted *Barfüszerkirche* "wenige Schritte von Gottfried Kellers Elternhaus entfernt."[19] It is definitely known that Keller saw one play performed on this stage, and, as Ermatinger says "Auch weitere Stücke mag Keller hier gehört haben."[20] If Keller saw one or more of Schiller's fiery dramas of freedom, as he very likely did, it would mean that Schiller and Schiller's freedom must have taken on a flesh-and-blood reality for the youth.

Secondly, Keller's earliest thoughts on freedom show indebtedness to Schiller's essays. To illustrate this, one may refer to a passage from Keller's diary of 1838 which shows a striking similarity in both terminology and content to Schiller's *Ueber Anmut und Würde*:

> Ein Mann ohne Tagebuch . . . ist was ein Weib ohne Spiegel. Dieses hört auf ein Weib zu sein, wenn es nicht mehr zu Gefallen strebt und seine Anmut vernachlässigt: es wird seiner Bestimmung dem Manne gegenüber untreu. Jener hört auf ein Mann zu sein, wenn er sich selbst nicht mehr beobachtet, und Erholung und Nahrung auszer sich sucht. Er verliert seine Haltung, seine Festigkeit, seinen Charakter, und wenn er seine geistige Selbständigkeit dahin gibt, so wird er ein Tropf. Diese Selbständigkeit kann aber nur bewahrt werden durch stetes Nachdenken über sich selbst. (*Ermatinger* II, 101)

In this passage Keller first discussed *Anmut* and concluded that it was the *Bestimmung* of woman. This is very similar to Schiller's treatment as Schiller also first concerned himself with *Anmut* in connection with the *Bestimmung* of man and woman, and had summed up: "Anmut wird also der Ausdruck weiblicher Tugend sein."[21] Keller had then discussed the fundamental importance to man of *geistige Selbständigkeit,* whereas Schiller went on to a consideration of *Würde* as the masculine virtue. The correspondence of *geistige Selbständigkeit* and *Würde* is obvious from Schiller's definition of *Würde* as the manifestation of "eines herrschenden Geistes"[22] and as the expression of *Geistesfreiheit.*[23] Keller concluded that man must strive for

---

[19] *Ermatinger* I, 28.
[20] *Ibid.*
[21] *Schillers Sämtliche Werke, Deut. Nat. Lit.*, Bd. 129, p. 97.
[22] *Ibid.*, p. 104.
[23] *Ibid.*, p. 102. "Beherrschung der Triebe durch die moralische Kraft ist Geistesfreiheit und Würde heiszt ihr Ausdruck in der Erscheinung."

geistige Selbständigkeit; and Schiller decided that since *Anmut* was for the present an unattainable ideal, *Würde* was the proper bearing of an honorable man.[24] Above and beyond these similarities, it is of conclusive importance to note that *Ueber Anmut und Würde* concerned itself with the persistent ideal of both the young and the mature Keller, namely, the conception of a freewill which did not violate natural law.

Significant evidence that Schiller influenced Keller's early attitude is also found in the letter of 1837 which contained Keller's first discussion of *Freiheit*. The tone of the first part of the letter, as well as the use of the concepts *Geschmack* and *Schönheit* indicates a familiarity with Schiller's *Briefe über die aesthetische Erziehung*:

> Er (der wahre Mensch) sei edel und einfach, aber einfach mit Geschmack, aus Achtung seiner selbst und nicht um andern zu gefallen! Den, der seinen Körper mit Absicht in einen schmutzigen Kittel steckt, verlache ich; denn, wenn der das Gefühl der Schönheit für sich nicht hat, so hat er's auch nicht für die Natur, und wenn er es für die Natur nicht hat, so hat er einen Risz in seinem Herzen, der ihn zum kleinen Menschen macht, ja sogar unter das Tier setzt, und wenn er sonst noch so gescheit wäre. (*Ermatinger* II, 5)

It is the following passage from the letter, however, that is of primary importance, because it contains ideas on freedom similar to those of Schiller, particularly as he formulated them in the first few pages of his essay *Ueber Naive und Sentimentalische Dichtung*:

> Ich mache einen groszen Unterschied zwischen dem, der die Natur nur um ihrer Formen, und dem der sie um ihrer innern Harmonie willen anbetet . . . Der Mensch, der der Natur und sich selbst angehört, bewahre in seiner Brust ein göttliches Gefühl von natürlichem Rechte, und auf der hellen hohen Stirn throne das hehre Bewusztsein der Freiheit! . . . Ich meine nicht die Freiheit des Pöbels, noch die politische, sondern jene Freiheit, die Gott eigen ist, und die den, der sie erkennt, keine schlechte Tat begehen läszt; aber die Erkenntnis dieser Freiheit wird nur erworben durch ein reines, denkendes Herz, das seine Bestimmung aufsucht in der Welten harmonischer Wechselbewegung. (*Ermatinger* II, 5-6)

A number of parallels may be drawn between this passage and Schiller's essay which bring out the similarity in phrasing,

---

[24] *Ibid*, pp. 109-113.

organization, and particularly, philosophy. Both men began with a discussion of the feelings which a fine or true person experienced in nature. To designate this person Schiller used the term "feinerer Mensch," and Keller used the term "wahrer Mensch." Both then went on to specify that the appreciation of nature did not refer to nature's outer beauty. Schiller said that this appreciation "richtet sich ganz und gar nicht nach der Schönheit der Formen"[25]; Keller stated: "Ich mache einen groszen Unterschied zwischen dem, der die Natur nur um ihrer Formen, und dem, der sie um ihrer innern Harmonie willen anbetet." Both indicated also that the appreciation was neither aesthetic nor purely intellectual, Schiller pointing out that man at times felt this deep reverence for nature "nicht weil sie unsern Sinnen wohltut, auch nicht, weil sie unsern Verstand oder Geschmack befriedigt, sondern blosz weil sie Natur ist," whereas Keller earlier in the letter[26] had indicated his preference for the enthusiast who worshipped the sun for its own sake to either the writer who merely praised the sun for its effect or the artist who eulogized the sun's beauty. Both writers showed furthermore that the reverence for nature to which they referred was a reflection of man's love for the idea inherent in nature, for the eternal natural order. Schiller had said: "Diese Art des Wohlgefallens an der Natur . . . ist ein moralisches. Es ist eine durch sie dargestellte Idee, die wir lieben." This idea was "das stille schaffende Leben, das ruhige Wirken aus sich selbst, das Dasein nach eignen Gesetzen."

Keller's interest in "innere Harmonie" has already been mentioned. That this inner harmony referred to the order in nature, which in turn reflected a divine ordering hand, is apparent from his early nature poems and from an essay of the same year.[27]

---

[25] *Ibid.*, pp. 342-344. Daraus erhellt, dasz diese Art des Wohlgefallens an der Natur kein ästhetisches, sondern ein moralisches ist: denn es wird durch eine Idee vermittelt, nicht unmittelbar durch Betrachtung erzeugt; auch richtet es sich ganz und gar nicht nach der Schönheit der Formen . . . Wir lieben in ihnen (life in nature) das stille schaffende Leben, das ruhige Wirken aus sich selbst, das Dasein nach eignen Gesetzen, die innere Notwendigkeit, die ewige Einheit mit sich selbst. Sie sind was wir waren, was wir w e r d e n   s o l l e n. Wir waren Natur wie sie, und unsere Kultur soll uns, auf dem Wege der Vernunft und der Freiheit, zur Natur zurückführen . . . Was Ihren Charakter ausmacht, ist gerade das, was dem unsrigen, zu seiner Vollendung mangelt; was uns von ihnen unterscheidet ist gerade das, was ihnen selbst zur Göttlichkeit fehlt. Wir sind frei und sie sind notwendig; wir wechseln, sie bleiben eins. Aber nur, wenn beides sich mit einander verbindet . . . wenn der Wille das Gesetz der Notwendigkeit frei befolgt und bei allem Wechsel der Phantasie die Vernunft ihre Regel behauptet, geht das Göttliche oder das Ideal hervor.
[26] *Ermatinger* II, 5.
[27] XIII, 35-70 (Buch der Natur). Cf. p. 17 in this study.

For both men again, the law of mankind was to progress from a state of nature to a state of voluntary acceptance of nature. Speaking of children, Schiller had said: "Sie sind was wir waren, was wir werden sollen." Keller expressed the idea of evolutionary progress to moral freedom within the framework of natural law more clearly in other early works and best in *Der Grüne Heinrich*,[28] but here his idea is clear enough from the statement that a true man must belong both to nature and to himself, and to acquire *Freiheit* had to seek his destiny in "der Welten harmonischer Wechselbewegung."

Personal freedom to heed one's moral responsibility within the limits of natural law was the ideal of both. Schiller spoke of "Freiheit in der Notwendigkeit" and Keller of "jene Freiheit, die keine schlechte Tat begehen läszt."[29] The ideal was to be realized through enlightenment. Schiller said that "die Bestimmung des Menschen (ist) Intelligenz!" and that "unsere Kultur auf dem Wege der Vernunft und Freiheit" would lead man back to a life of freedom in necessity. Keller likewise felt that the man who gained freedom would have to be a sincere thinker, "ein reines, denkendes Herz." It is important to note that here more than elsewhere Schiller strove to reconcile natural and moral law, a problem with which Keller concerned himself all his life and expressed best in *Das Sinngedicht*.

These comparisons between Keller's diary of 1838 and the letter of 1837 on the one hand and Schiller's essays on the other show that in a purely formal sense the adolescent Keller agreed quite closely with Schiller in his conception of an ordered nature, a purposeful progress in human development, the guiding function of the intellect, and the necessity of voluntary acceptance of nature. The importance of the letter of 1837, especially, cannot be overemphasized, as every aspect of the concept of freedom mentioned there was retained, developed, and clarified in Keller's mature philosophy. The letter thus shows both the early origin of Keller's consistent interest in moral freedom,

---

[28] Cf. pp. 59-63 in this study.
[29] Cf. letter of 1837, *Ermatinger* II, 5.

and the relation of that consistent interest to Schiller's ideal.[30] Maturity and the probable realization that Schiller's philosophy was based on a dualism did not decrease Keller's respect for Schiller or for his ideal of moral freedom.[31] Throughout his life Keller had nothing but words of praise for both. His first direct reference to Schiller's freedom was in an essay of 1841, *Vermischte Gedanken über die Schweiz*, which had as its theme the need for intellectual clarity to preserve political freedom.[32] He praised Schiller for his defense of the inviolate freedom of the spirit:

> Während Schiller mit der ganzen Glut seines Herzens die feurigen Worte singt: "Der Mensch ist frei geschaffen, ist frei, und wäre er in Ketten geboren!" läszt der Geheimrat von Goethe in nobler Behaglichkeit seinen Tasso sagen: "der Mensch ist nicht geboren frei zu sein, und für den Edlen gibt's kein gröszer Glück als einem Fürsten, den er liebt, zu dienen."[33]

In 1844, Keller wrote a fiery sonnet in praise of the writers who fought for the freedom of the intellect.[34] In the dedication, Schiller's name came first. In 1847, Keller summarized his philosophy in the poem *Erkenntnis* in which the key-line read, "... tu was du nicht lassen kannst,"[35] a wording very similar to the familiar quotation from *William Tell*: "Ich hab' getan, was ich nicht lassen konnte." The first longer work after the experience of 1849 was the poem, *Der Apotheker von Chamounix*

---

[30] The views Keller expressed in the letter of 1837 were undoubtedly his own, that is though originally taken from Schiller, consciously or otherwise, they had been "längst ... zu eigen gemacht." This is apparent from the natural development of thought in the passage and from the unrestrained admixture of philosophic terms borrowed from Schiller with terms taken from the romantic writers.

Schiller seems to have prepared Keller for his enthusiastic acceptance of Feuerbach in two ways. First, Schiller helped to provide Keller with the basic attitude which had so much in common with the nature doctrine of Feuerbach. Secondly, Schiller's terms *Innere Notwendigkeit, geistige Freiheit, Bestimmung*, etc., were also key-words for Feuerbach, who differed little in his logical procedure or terminology from the earlier German idealists, so that when Feuerbach awakened these latent ideas in Keller, they were welcome old friends.

[31] Cf. H. Reichert, *A Comparison of the Philosophies of Schiller and Keller, Monatshefte*, April 1947. Keller could still write of Schiller and Goethe in a letter to Hettner of 1850 (*Ermatinger* II, 269) that their works although outmoded contained "innere Wahrheit."

[32] Hans M. Kriesi, *op. cit.*, appendix, p. 245. In the essay Keller had also said: "Nur dadurch, dasz wir jeden guten Gedanken in uns aufnehmen, komme er von wem er wolle, dasz wir die Wahrheit an jeder Partei zu schätzen wissen, dasz wir in unseren Gegnern nicht die Personen, sondern nur die falschen Grundsätze hassen ..."

[33] *Ibid.*, p. 245.

[34] XIII, 156. (*Kampfsonette*)

[35] XVi, 53.

(1853), which was a strong attack on *Willkür*.³⁶ Heine was made the arch-representative of arbitrary freewill and Schiller a champion of Keller's views. Schiller was made to reproach Heine for his arbitrary conduct:

> Feurig wuszt ich auch zu singen
> Aber ohne mich zu brennen!³⁷

Der Grüne Heinrich (1855), though it did not directly praise Schiller's ideal, had words of praise for "seine gleichmäszige Glut und Reinheit des Gedankens und der Sprache."³⁸ The *Prolog* of 1859³⁹ revealed most clearly the identification in Keller's mind of Schiller's ideal with his own. Schiller's *Schönheit* was endowed with all the attributes of intellectual clarity. It gave power and harmony to thought. It alone led to the highest freedom and maintained that freedom. Keller was convinced that Schiller's ultimate goal was likewise a mature and free intellect:

> Und Schiller lehrt uns so zu handeln, dasz wenn morgen
> Ein Gott uns jählings aus dem Dasein triebe,
> Ein fertig Geistesbild bestehen bliebe.
> (I, 269, *Gesammelte Gedichte*).

At the banquet connected with the Schiller Festival for which the *Prolog* was written, Keller gave a speech, the theme of which was Schiller's *Befreiungsidee*.⁴⁰

Keller expressed consistent praise and admiration for Schiller the man. The highest compliment Keller could pay to anyone was given Schiller in the *Apotheker von Chamounix*: his life

---

[36] Keller's use of the term *Willkür* should not be permitted to confuse recognition of the similar pattern of his and Schiller's thought. Despite the fact that for Schiller *Willkür* referred to the most praiseworthy attribute of man, and for Keller *Willkür* was man's least desirable trait, the difference is only superficial and does not reflect a difference in attitude but in use of words. Keller used the term *Willkür* as Feuerbach had used it in opposition to *Notwendigkeit* which reflected the ethical aspect of Feuerbach's philosophy. As was indicated above, Keller had taken over the Feuerbachian terminology in *Der Grüne Heinrich* and retained that terminology thereafter though he came to use the terms less frequently for artistic reasons. Thus *Willkür* for Keller meant conduct at variance with the pattern of moral conduct set up by nature, and implied an absence of freewill. Schiller, on the other hand, used *Willkür* to designate man's free action, but did not include action not in accordance with "dem höchsten Endzweck" or "dem Gesetz der Notwendigkeit." Such arbitrary action Schiller relegated to the undesirable concept of *blinde Willkür* which approximated Keller's use of *Willkür*.

[37] XVi, 244. (*Nachgelassene Gedichte*). Keller had let Schiller go on to say: "Allzugut ist gar nicht gut, Golden ist die Mittelstrasze!"

[38] XVI, 84.

[39] Cf. pp. 75-77 in this study.

[40] *Ermatinger* I, 386.

had been the expression of inner necessity.[41] The warmth of the praise expressed in *Der Grüne Heinrich* can be appreciated best by one closely familiar with Keller. Choosing Schiller as an example of "ein wahres und vernünftiges Leben," Keller said of him:

> Dieser, nur das tuend was er nicht lassen konnte ... veredelte sich unablässig von innen heraus und sein Leben war nichts anderes als die Erfüllung seines innersten Wesens, die folgerechte und krystallreine Arbeit der Wahrheit und des Idealen, die in ihm und seiner Zeit lagen. (XIX, 81)

Keller felt that the merit of Schiller's "ehrliches, klares und wahres Arbeitsleben" had showed itself most clearly in the success of Schiller's ideas and works after his death.[42]

In the *Prolog* of 1859 Keller had said of Schiller:

> Und wo im weiten Reich des deutschen Wortes,
> Drei Männer sind, die nicht am Staube kleben,
> Da denken sie bewegt an Friedrich Schiller
> Und mit ihm an das Beste, was sie kennen!
> (I, 265)

The essay *Am Mythenstein* (1861) expressed admiration for the writer of *William Tell,* who in his deep understanding of life had grasped the true nature of the Swiss people.[43] After 1861, Keller referred to Schiller in his writings only as a literary standard from which to criticize contemporaries.[44] However, his continued admiration for Schiller was attested to by his friend and biographer, Jakob Baechthold, who tells how the aged Keller vigorously defended Schiller against the strong onesided praise for Goethe.[45] As late as 1887, Keller voiced indirect admiration for Schiller when he wrote to Widmann his pleasure and embarrassment at having the latter, in a review of *Martin Salander,* compare that work with *William Tell.*[46]

---

[41] XVi, 244. "Nötig war mir diese Weise . . ."
[42] XIX, 81.
[43] Cf. fn. 48, p. 109 in this study. *Am Mythenstein,* pp. 47-48.
[44] *Ermatinger* III, 70. From this vantage point he blasted Grillparzer's *Jüdin von Toledo* in 1873 and J. V. Widmann's writings in 1879 (III, 294).
[45] *Ibid.,* I, 528. "Von den sogenannten Klassikern staunte er vor allem Schiller an . . . Wenn die einseitige Lobpreisung Goethes so weiter gehe, meinte er zu einer Zeit, da Schiller stark hinter jenen zurücktreten muszte, so fange er eine Verschwörung an. Einst, nach dem Lesen einer Rezension, worin Keller stark gelobt war, rief er aus: "Wer ist unsereiner gegen Schiller, der alles in allem war, ein groszer Dichter, sein eigener Verleger und Buchhändler, sogar der Verpacker der Horen!"
[46] *Ibid.,* III, 517.

To conclude, facts have been presented to show that Keller derived his early conception of freedom not from the romantic writers but from Schiller (especially from a work by Schiller which emphasized the importance and goodness of natural law), that Keller throughout his life consistently admired Schiller, and felt, even in his maturity, an ideological bond with Schiller. By supporting the thesis that Keller, when only a youth, had already conceived of *Freiheit* as a kind of *Freiheit in der Notwendigkeit*, not in the Kantian sense of Schiller, to be sure, but as a freedom which contained the idea of obedience to natural law, these facts further weaken the claim that Feuerbach "changed" Keller. By testifying to Keller's esteem for Schiller and Schiller's ideal, before and after 1849, they show that Keller's *Weltanschauung* was characterized by consistency rather than by change.

APPENDIX

A BRIEF SURVEY OF THE CRITICAL STUDIES ON KELLER'S PHILOSOPHY

For all its variety of conclusions, the critical literature on Keller has, in general, over-emphasized his early romanticism, has ignored, subordinated, or misinterpreted the nonpolitical implications of his early conception of freedom, has failed to integrate this conception with his total early outlook, and consequently has failed to realize the consistent and personal nature of Keller's *Weltanschauung*. This was possible because, despite their characteristic divergence of opinion, the studies on Keller's *Weltanschauung* also reveal a tenacious adherence to a few set ways of thinking, to a few established methods of approach and analysis, which have funnelled their conclusions into restricted channels. These established methods are three in number and may be termed romantic-realistic, political, and dynamic.

The romantic-realistic method is the most important since the largest number of studies have employed it. This method deals with romanticism and realism in Keller's views, either as successive stages in his development or as concurrent phenomena. Keller himself, when barely thirty years old, already fathered the idea that romanticism and realism were successive stages in his outlook by emphasizing in his autobiographical novel, *Der Grüne Heinrich*, the transition in the views of the hero from *Willkür* and romantic subjectivity to *Notwendigkeit* and realistic objectivity. The thesis that romanticism and realism existed concurrently in Keller's attitude was developed by Otto Ludwig who both formulated the concept of poetic realism[1] and applied it to Keller's works. For example, Ludwig spoke of the poetic realism in *Frau Regel Amrain* as follows:

> Es ist die Romantik, der das zähe, gesunde, schweizerische Phlegma den Schwerpunkt und die feste Leiblichkeit gibt, die unserer deutschen Romantik fehlte oder, wenn man es so nennen will, die poeti-

---

[1] Merker-Stammler defines poetic realism as follows: Man bezeichnet so die Literaturströmung, die seit der Mitte des Jahrhunderts, deutlicher von da bis gegen das Ende der 80er Jahre andauert. Das Wesen des Poetischen Realismus liegt in seiner vorbehaltenen Wirklichkeitsschilderung. Der Zusatz "poetisch" will aber besagen, dasz es dabei nicht auf eine pessimistische Zersetzung des Lebens abgesehen sei, das vielmehr in seinem tiefsten Grunde bejaht werden soll. (Merker-Stammler, *Reallexikon*, III, 4.)

sche Wahrheit. Mit Hebbel verglichen, der ebenfalls auf ein glühendes Kolorit hinarbeitet, ist Keller Fleisch, mit Keller verglichen ist Hebbel von Holz.[2]

That Ludwig might well have had Keller more in mind than any other writer when he formulated the concept of poetic realism is apparent from the fact that Keller is usually recognized to be the perfect representative of poetic realism:

> Seine Dichtung steht, ihre Phasen spiegelnd, ihre verschiedenen Ausstrahlungen, in der Breite und Tiefe ausschöpfend, nicht nur im Mittelpunkte der Strömung, sie enthält zugleich auch die Formel für ihr innerstes Lebensgefühl. (Merker-Stammler, *Reallexikon*, III, 5)

The romantic-realistic method has produced a number of enlightening studies on Keller which have shown with great clarity the double aspect of his outlook, but it has some failings. It was so tempting for scholars to stress Keller's transition from romanticism to realism, as Keller himself had done, and then to correlate the transition in attitude with the changing *Zeitgeist* of the century, that persistent aspects of outlook common to both his earlier and later *Weltanschauung* were neglected. The emphasis on transition also induced several scholars to limit their studies to one period of Keller's "changing" outlook, either to the early "romantic" period, to the "realistic" period of his maturity, or to the "naturalistic" period of his advanced years, so that these studies add only indirectly to an understanding of the permanent aspects of Keller's attitude.

The second approach concerned itself with Keller the political man, was dominant during his own life-time, and experienced a brief renascence at the beginning of both world wars. Its contribution was to reveal Keller's life-long interest in freedom. However, as the studies of this group interested themselves primarily in Keller's political views, the *Freiheit* with which they were concerned was solely political freedom.

A third group of studies, in contradistinction to the preceding two, focussed their attention exclusively on the dynamic essence of Keller's *Weltanschauung*. They dealt with the "inner experience" which they felt gave Keller's works their indefinable vitality. The value of these studies lies in the attention they drew to the unchanging core of Keller's attitude, his dynamic,

---

[2] Quoted by Gleichen-Russwurm, *Gottfried Kellers Weltanschauung*, p. 68.

optimistic spirit. Though the more recent of these studies[3] specifically claimed to be studies of *Weltanschauung,* they concentrated solely on a discussion of Keller's inner experience without showing with sufficient clarity how Keller expressed and visualized that experience. They are typical studies in the Dilthey manner, and subordinate a discussion of *Weltanschauung* to a demonstration of the degree to which *Weltanschauung* was experienced.

In order to lend full validity to the contention that the Keller literature has been routed into too narrow channels of investigation, the existing studies dealing with Keller's *Weltanschauung* will now be considered in their relation to the established methods of approach, beginning with the romantic-realistic method.

In 1883, six years before Keller's death, Otto Brahm published a book entitled *Gottfried Keller* which echoed the opinion voiced earlier by Otto Ludwig and which brought out the two phases of Keller's style and attitude. On the one hand, Keller's Swiss heritage was seen to reflect his realism. On the other, his adherence to German culture was felt to reflect his romanticism.

In 1893, Jakob Baechthold published his three-volume biography of Keller, which, though it purported to let Keller speak for himself through his letters, was so arranged that the Feuerbach experience of 1849 stood forth as the turning point in Keller's life.

In 1899, the distinguished French scholar Fernand Baldensperger followed Baechthold's lead and devoted a book of over five hundred pages to Keller's life and works. Baldensperger also considered the Feuerbach incident to be of crucial importance to Keller's mature outlook, but was not misled to believe that contact with Feuerbach brought about a complete change in Keller's views:

> Ce fut moins, peut-être, une conversion absolue, le soudain bouleversement d'un esprit, qu'une façon de cristallization complète d'éléments épars qui s'organizent et s'agglomèrent sous l'effet d'un agent nouveau. (*op. cit.,* p. 90)
>
> Même la grande crise morale de son existence, celle que détermina Feuerbach en 1849, a été moins pour lui une soudaine trans-

---

[3] To be discussed below, pp. 155-158.

formation qu'une sorte de maturation et de confirmation, et n'a point modifier les régions profondes de son être. (p. 370)

In the second part of his work, Baldensperger undertook to analyze the five dominant aspects of Keller's writing. The first aspect was entitled "l'helvetisme," under which he discussed Keller's nationalism and realism, in the manner of Ludwig and Brahm. The second aspect was "le romantisme." Baldensperger felt that even Keller's mature views were to some extent affiliated with romantic ideas:

Il faut noter qu'en face des phénomènes de la nature, l'émotion de Keller ne suit pas la tradition romantique . . .[4]

Il y a ainsi, dans l'oeuvre de Keller, un certain nombre de notions qui sont, non point personnifiées, mais révélées à demi, avec une sorte de charme mystique que le romantisme fervent d'un Novalis ou d'un Shelley n'eût point réprouvé.[5]

The other three aspects were *le sens de la vue, l'humour,* and *le style.* Though Baldensperger was fully aware that *Selbstbefreiung* was the theme of *Der Apotheker von Chamounix* and other works,[6] the scope of his undertaking left him unable and unwilling to deal in detail with Keller's outlook. Thus, in his discussion of *Der Grüne Heinrich,* he summarized the important philosophical section which began at the end of the third and included the whole of the fourth book, by stating that it was a complicated treatment of Heinrich's intellectual maturing which was "souvent pauvre de charme" (p. 139). As for Keller's early conception of freedom, Baldensperger took this as solely political in nature and not worthy of detailed discussion since political themes were incapable of artistic treatment.[7] As a result, Baldensperger's sympathetic, penetrating, and comprehensive work, though a major contribution to Keller criticism, added little to an understanding of Keller's life-long interest in moral freedom and enlightenment.

In 1909 there appeared the first of three studies dealing with the romantic side of Keller's style and attitude. Paul R. Meintel's *Gottfried Keller und die Romantik* traced Keller's relation to seventeen romantic writers and made much of a brief essay

---

[4] Fernand Baldensperger, *Gottfried Keller, Sa Vie et Ses Oeuvres.* p. 408.
[5] *Ibid.,* p. 409.
[6] *Ibid.,* p. 362.
[7] *Ibid.,* p. 345.

Die Romantik und die Gegenwart, (*Eine Grille*), written by Keller in 1849, in which Keller had expressed sympathy for the "unschuldige, reinliche Romantik" and had drawn a sharp distinction between such romanticism and the "systematische Romantik der Reaktion":

> Ich meine nicht die systematische Romantik der Reaktion, noch die blutschauerliche Romantik der Franzosen, auch nicht die subjektif-ironische Partie der Schule; ich denke nur an die unschuldige, reinliche Romantik an sich, wie sie sich in den liebenswürdigeren Aeuszerungen der deutschen Schule dargestellt hat, wie sie im "Oktavian" und anderen Gedichten Tiecks, im "Ofterdingen," in den helleren Seiten Arnims, in einigen Märchen Brentanos und in Uhlands Balladen und Romanzen lebt.[8]

Meintel presented convincing data to show romantic literary influence on the young Keller, but selected and cut quotations somewhat arbitrarily to bring out Keller's interest in romanticism. Quoting two long paragraphs in which Keller praised romanticism as the best expression of the past, for having awakened and captured the poetic mood of the Rhineland, Meintel omitted the important words beginning the second paragraph, "Ich sage, bisher," which had indicated that romanticism held no value for the present, and ended his citation just prior to the line, "Gegenwärtig aber ringt alle Welt nach einem neuen Sein und nach einem neuen Gewande."

In 1912 Frieda Jaeggi, in *Gottfried Keller und Jean Paul,* undertook an even more specialized study to show Keller's debt to romanticism, and discussed the literary and to some extent the philosophical influence of Jean Paul on Keller's early writing and on *Der Grüne Heinrich.*

Anna Weimann-Bischoff's study, *Gottfried Keller und die Romantik* (1917) was the final and most comprehensive study of Keller's relationship to romanticism. With scholarly restraint, Miss Bischoff admitted that no direct influence of romantic writers on Keller's thought could be shown, but felt nevertheless that "manches in seinen ethischen Bekenntnissen stimmt mit ihrem (der älteren Romantik) groszen und idealen Streben überein" (p. 94). The study concluded that Keller was "Ueberwinder und Vollender der Romantik" since he had accomplished

---

[8] pp. 16-17 in Meintel's study. Keller's essay may be found in Jakob Baechthold, *Gottfried Kellers Leben. Seine Briefe und Tagebücher,* I, 462.

"eine organische Verschmelzung von Romantik und Realistik" (p. 45).

In the same year that Meintel discussed Keller's early debt to romanticism, Agnes Waldhausen published a work entitled *Gottfried Kellers Grüner Heinrich in seinen Beziehungen zu Goethes Dichtung und Wahrheit,* in which she showed the similarity of the mature Keller's conception of nature to that of Goethe.

A dissertation by Gustav Müller-Gschwend, *Gottfried Keller als lyrischer Dichter* (1910), introduced a short-lived revival of interest in Keller's lyrics. This work showed its dependence on the romantic-realistic approach by dividing its material chronologically into three groups of which the first stressed Keller's romanticism, the second his realism, and the third the combination of the two in the lyrics of his old age:

> Von der Romantik ausgegangen, ist er immer individueller und echter geworden, und wenn sich auch in der Phraseologie noch manche der prunkhaften, romantischen Naturphanomäne forterhalten haben, so ist doch die Stoffwahl entschiedener auf Schlichtes gerichtet. Dies Urteil über seine Naturlyrik darf man für die ganze Lyrik der zweiten Periode verallgemeinern: *die Spuren der Romantik beschränken sich zumeist auf einzelne Ausdrücke und treten stark hinter dem Eigengut zurück.* (p. 33) (my italics)

> Für seine Spätlingsgedichte gilt am meisten in seiner gesamten lyrischen Entwicklung seine eigene Definition des Schönen als der "mit Fülle vorgetragenen Wahrheit" ... Er suchte oft peinlich das Reale lange "bevor er Zola las" ... er empfand wohl das wachsende Bedürfnis der Zeit nach strengerem Wirklichkeitssinn und *legte sich eine geistige Zucht auf,* während seine ursprüngliche Anlage und die Erinnerungen seiner literarischen Jugend *ein freieres Walten der Phantasie begünstigten.* (p. 47) (my italics)

Müller-Gschwend took note of Keller's interest in *Freiheit* in the lyrics of 1843-1847, but discussed it only briefly as a purely political concept.

Two further studies on Keller's lyrics were printed in 1911, both using the romantic-realistic approach. Ernst Korrodi's *Gottfried Keller ein deutscher Lyriker* emphasized the change in Keller's views much in the manner of Müller-Gschwend:

> Seine Gedichte sind die Dokumente des Wandels seiner Weltanschauung vom Unsterblichkeitsglauben in dessen Verneinung and der milden Versöhnung dieser Gegensätze in der spätherbstlichen

Lyrik. Die Gedichte von 1846 und von 1851 verhalten sich zueinander wie zwei Disputanten pro et contra. (p. 79)

Korrodi's real contribution was his belief that the admixture of lyric and epic present in the old poet, was present in the young writer as well; speaking of the latter, Korrodi said:

> Im Grunde seiner Seele bleibt er immer Fabulierer und Erzähler und köstlicher Erfinder. Selbst seine Gedichte haben zwei Augen: ein lyrisches und ein episches. (p. 32)

Korrodi's conclusion that Keller's epic-lyric dualism reflected his spiritual adherence to both the Swiss and German cultures brings to mind Ludwig, Brahm, and Baldensperger:

> Sie (Keller's lyrics) sind der Spiegel seines geistigen Doppellebens; des Schweizers als freudigen Zugehörigen einer bestimmten Stammesart und einer treu gepflegten Kultur, des Deutschen, als freudigen Anteilhabers aller Segnungen des groszen deutschen Kulturganzen und der groszen deutschen Literatur. (p. 133)

Philipp Witkop's short work on *Gottfried Keller als Lyriker* (1911) dealt with the philosophical significance of Keller's lyrics. His thesis, that Keller's shift from subjectivity to objectivity was reflected in his lyrical style, was new only in its terminology. Witkop first discussed the subjectivity of the early lyrics:

> Aber er hatte kaum ein Dutzend Seiten geschrieben, als *seine unerlöste Subjektivität* jäh zur eigensten Form durchbrach. (p. 19) (my italics)

This subjectivity was ended by the Heidelberg experience:

> In Heidelberg schliesz Keller seinen zweiten Gedichtband ab— und mit ihm seine Jugend, mit ihm *alle Subjektivität* . . . (p. 22) (my italics)

> Bis in die tiefsten Gründe seines Weltgefühls ist das Bedürfnis nach *epischer Objektivität* gedrungen . . . Er wollte aller Subjektivität entsagen, Feuerbach verwies ihm die höchste Subjektivität des Menschen: Gott. (p. 23) (my italics)

With the objectivization of his attitude, Keller lost his lyric talent:

> Mit dieser urgründigen Objektivierung seines Wesens und Wollens ist der Lyriker in Keller vernichtet. Fünfundzwanzig Jahre später schreibt er zwar auf einmal noch ein Dutzend Gedichte, aber

alle auszer einem sind epischen, erzählenden Charakters. (pp. 24-25)

Both Witkop and Korrodi discussed the early *Freiheitsgedichte* as purely political poetry. Korrodi, however, recognized the philosophic implications of the *Prolog* of 1859 and felt Keller had, in that work, approached Schiller's conception of moral freedom.

The first important contribution by the eminent Keller scholar, Emil Ermatinger, was an essay which appeared in 1912. Entitled *Gottfried Kellers Weltanschauung*, it reflected clearly the prevalent romantic-realistic approach. The study was divided into two parts. The first part emphasized the romantic aspects of Keller's attitude till 1849: romantic caprice (*Witz*), lyric nature poetry, and nature-worship. The second part discussed Keller's attitude after 1849, which was summed up as "physischer Pantheismus." Ermatinger at this time maintained that the "sinnlich-geistig" conception of the world held by the mature Keller was given him by the realist Goethe and not by Ludwig Feuerbach, who, Ermatinger felt, had only "burst the cocoon" of latent ideas:

> Diese polare sinnlich-geistige Betrachtung der Welt ist auch die Frucht von Gottfried Kellers Goethe Erlebnis gewesen. (*Wissen und Leben*, 1911, p. 340)

In 1916 Ermatinger revised Baechthold's biography to produce the classic reference work on Keller. Ermatinger's biography, organized on the same pattern as his earlier essay, traced the development in Keller's attitude from romanticism to realism; Chapter XV, for example, had the caption: "Der Grabgesang auf die Romantik und die vaterländischen Erzählungen." This work discussed Keller's lyrics of freedom solely in connection with the political struggles of the times and dealt with his nature lyrics in terms of romantic influence. The earlier conviction that Keller's mature conception of nature had come from Goethe rather than Feuerbach was now given up, and the new principle of "sittlich-sinnlich" applied to an analysis of the later works.

In 1919, in *Gottfried Keller an der Scheide zweier Zeitalter*, Ermatinger discussed the "Zwiespalt in des Dichters eigener Seele" between romanticism and realism, and analysed *Der Grüne Heinrich* as the "gesetzmäszige Auseinandersetzung zwischen der romantischen Künstlerwelt und den praktischen Forderungen des neuzeitlichen Realismus."[9]

In 1920, in *Gottfried Kellers Lebensglaube,* and in 1933, in his discussion of Keller in *Dichtung und Geistesleben der deutschen Schweiz,* Ermatinger continued to stress Keller's transition from romanticism to realism. Two sample paragraphs from the latter work reveal the emphasis placed on Feuerbach and transition:

> Seine ersten Bilder, seine ersten Gedichte zeigen, dasz er mit einem Uebermasz romantizierender Phantasie die Natur immer wieder verunstaltet, in der Meinung sie durch etwas Geistreiches verschönern, interessanter machen zu müssen.[10]
>
> Natur ist Fülle—Natur ist Ordnung. Für Feuerbach ist sie beides, und Keller lernt durch ihn den Gegensatz seiner Veranlagung nach dieser Doppelformel deuten . . .Wir sehen sie (die Doppelformel) in der Reihe der nun entstehenden Dichtungen als Idee wirken, wobei der Begriffsgegensatz Natursinnlichkeit-sittliche Ordnung in den mannigfaltigsten Farbenspielen sich abwandelt.[11]

Ermatinger is probably more interested than any other individual in Keller and has made numerous and excellent contributions to the critical literature. His emphasis, however, on the transitional nature of Keller's *Weltanschauung* has never permitted him to deal adequately with the problem of Keller's early realism. Keller's youthful conception of *Freiheit* meant no more for Ermatinger than political freedom, as is clearly shown in his biography of 1916[12] and in his study, *Gottfried Keller an der Scheide zweier Zeitalter* (1919):

> Der ewige Gegensatz zwischen Ideal und Wirklichkeit brannte als Drang nach der Freiheit in ihm, *wie in Herwegh* und *Freiligrath*... Er dichtete seine leidenschaftlichen *politischen Bekenntnisse*... (*Krisen und Probleme,* p. 270) (my italics)

In his discussion of Keller's early lyrics in *Dichtung und Geistesleben der deutschen Schweiz* (1933), Ermatinger still associated Keller's ideal of *Freiheit* with political freedom:

> In der Lyrik hat das jugendliche Temperament des Freiheitskämpfers seinen ersten leidenschaftlichen Ausbruch gefunden. Schon

---

[9] Emil Ermatinger, *Krisen und Probleme der neueren deutschen Dichtung* (collected essays and speeches), p. 275.
[10] *Dichtung und Geistesleben der deutschen Schweiz,* p. 629.
[11] *Ibid.,* p. 631.
[12] *Gottfried Kellers Leben, Briefe, und Tagebücher* I, pp. 131, 143, and 145.

> das erste Gedicht des Schicksalsjahres 1843 . . . bekennt: "Die Fahne, der ich folgen musz, ist weisz und purpurrot." (p. 632)

Till recently, Ermatinger was of the opinion that ethical ideas borrowed en masse from Feuerbach had impeded Keller's intellectual and spiritual growth:

> So erstaunlich reich an Gehalt und Form dieses Schaffen der Jahre 1850-1855 ist, man darf sich doch heute der Tatsache nicht verschlieszen, dasz das völlige Bekenntnis des Dichters zum Materialismus *zugleich einen vorzeitigen Abbruch seines geistigen Wachstums bedeutet.* (*Krisen und Probleme*, p. 266) (my italics)

From the earlier "bewegten Ideenmasse"[13] Keller had retained only the ideas "des schweizerischen Bürgertums":

> Die auf den "Grünen Heinrich" folgenden Erzählungen von den "Leuten von Seldwyla" und den "Sieben Legenden" bis zu den "Züricher Novellen" und dem "Sinngedicht" *stellen Probleme und Konflikte des eigentlichen Lebens dar.* (*Krisen und Probleme*, p. 276) (my italics)

Walter Schmiele, literary critic of the *Literaturblatt* of the *Frankfurter Zeitung* expressed the consensus of modern opinion when he spoke disparagingly of the "heute freilich bei den Einsichtigen schon preisgegebene Meinung, das Demokratisch-Bürgerliche weise auf die Ursprünge seines (Kellers) Wesens hin."[14]

However, Ermatinger must also be given his due, and it must be said that already in *Gottfried Kellers Lebensglaube* (1920) he had stressed Keller's deep religious experience. Furthermore, in an article in *Die Tatwelt*, "Die Religion Gottfried Kellers" (1940), Ermatinger devaluated considerably the influence of Feuerbach, terming his influence, as we have done, "ein logisch klärender":

> "Aber man musz sich doch hüten, den Einflusz des weitwirkenden Materialisten auf den Dichter zu überschätzen, und wer diesen schlechthin einen Feuerbachianer nennt, würde ihm schon darum unrecht tun, weil jene persönliche religiöse Grundhaltung Kellers, das Bewusztsein des Besitzes des Glaubens als einer lebendigen innern Kraft, alle b e g r i f f l i c h e Formulierung des Glaubensinhaltes grundsätzlich ablehnt, ob sie nun von der Theologie oder

---

[13] *Krisen und Probleme*, p. 275.
[14] *Frankfurter Zeitung Literaturblatt*, "Gottfried Keller" Sonntag, 19. Juni 1938, p. 8. Cf. also Lydia Baer's study on Ludwig Klages, *Journal of English and German Philology* XL (1941), 91-139.

> der Philosophie unternommen werde. Man wird also sagen müssen: Der Einflusz Feuerbachs ist vor allem ein logisch klärender gewesen. Er hat den letzten Rest der Vorstellung eines veralteten und unfruchtbar gewordenen Idealismus in ihm beseitigt und damit den persönlichen Glaubensbegriff völlig von den Elementen einer konventionellen Denküberlieferung befreit, heisze sie nun christliche Kirchenlehre oder philosophischer Idealismus." (p. 72)

As yet, Ermatinger has not attempted to discuss anew the tenets of Keller's outlook.

Probably the most painstaking study of Keller's philosophical views was made in 1913 by Hans Dünnebier in his study *Gottfried Keller und Ludwig Feuerbach*. Dünnebier recognized that Keller's early views on freedom had philosophical implications and that certain features of his early outlook were "unromantic" and prepared the way for his later beliefs.[15] Yet Dünnebier felt that the letter of 1837 reflected a completely romantic attitude[16] and that Keller's pantheism of the 1840's was still sufficiently different from his views of the 1850's to warrant terming the transition a radical change:

> Diese Weltanschauung, wie sie bisher ihre charakteristischen Seiten hervorgekehrt hat, vom Jüngling begründet, vom Mann geprüft, und aufs neue beschworen, sollte *binnen einem Vierteljahr einer vollständigen Umwälzung unterliegen*, bewirkt durch denselben Philosophen, über den Keller jetzt, Ende des Jahres 1848 den Stab brach, durch Ludwig Feuerbach. (p. 49) (my italics)

This study revealed its adherence to the romantic-realistic approach also in its chapter headings. Chapter I was entitled "Jugendromantik," Chapter IV, "Feuerbach," and Chapter V, "Romantik und Realismus." Nine chapters were devoted to the thesis that Feuerbach had caused the complete shift in Keller's ideas in 1849. Keller's interest in enlightenment was seen to be derived from Feuerbach's zeal for *Selbsterkenntnis* (p. 125).

Edward F. Hauch's study, *Gottfried Keller as a Democratic Idealist* (1916), reflected the prevalent approach as it sought to show the "development of his (Keller's) democratic thinking, and to define and outline his own peculiar type of democratic

---

[15] Cf. p. 51, fn. 3.
[16] Dünnebier, *op. cit.*, p. 2. *Eine Nacht auf dem Uto* expressed "alle verworrene sehnsüchtige Gefühle eines schwärmerischen Herzens" (p. 3). Speaking of the letter of 1838, "Das geforderte 'ruhige Anschauen der Natur' bedeutet keineswegs objektives Betrachten der Welt, entspricht erst recht nicht der tiefen Ehrfurcht vor den Dingen, die den Dichter später erfüllt."

idealism in its various aspects" by "tracing out his intimate affinity with all three of these main and vital currents ("romantic, propagandist, and realistic") of German literature" (p. 4). Hauch's first chapter dealt with Keller as a propagandist, and *Freiheit* was conceived of as purely political freedom. His second chapter, "Romanticism to Realism; religious ideals," discussed in orthodox fashion the early nature lyrics and the problem of God and immortality. The third chapter, "Realism; educational ideals," was a lucid analysis of Keller's ideas on education, and revealed clearly for the first time the importance which Keller attributed to education and an "independent" mind, though Hauch considered this intellectual independence solely in its political and social ramifications.[17]

Max Hochdorf's *Gottfried Keller im europäischen Gedanken* (1919) differed considerably from preceding studies, but still paid homage to the romantic-realistic approach. This critic's thesis was that Keller had evolved in his outlook from romanticism to mysticism to naturalism, and he correlated this evolution not with the trend in German but with the trend in French literature. Hochdorf felt that from 1838 till after the conception of the original *Grüner Heinrich* (1855), Keller had stood strongly under the influence of Honoré Balzac. Balzac's two stories *Das Unbekannte Meisterwerk* and *Die Erforschung des Absoluten* had appealed to Keller both for their element of "Wahrheitsdichtung" and for their "Romantik und Kolportage." The influence of Balzac's romanticism could still be seen in the conclusion of the original *Grüner Heinrich*:

> Doch solche Energie im Zerstören des Menschen ist ein gut Stück der Kolportagenphantasie Balzacs, die sich nur ausweiten und austoben will um jeden Preis. Je phantastischer eine Sache ist, desto mehr leuchtet sie dem jungen Keller ein. Und Keller ist ein Jüngling, dem das Letzte des Leides eher einleuchtet als die Wahrscheinlichkeit des höchsten Glückes. *Darum schon kann das Ende der Balzacschen Alchimistengeschichte nicht aus seinem Gedächtnis geschwunden sein, als er das Ende des grünen Heinrich bedenkt,* den er ja auf eine willkürliche und tragische Art einem frühen Tod entgegentreiben will. (p. 39) (my italics)

---

[17] Hauch made the following statement, but only developed it as indicated above: "Heinrich's mind at last becomes clarified and *independent*" (p. 63) (my italics).

In 1849, however, Keller had thrown off the influence of Balzac's romanticism. Not Feuerbach, but the futile love for Johanna Kapp had been the motivating factor:[18]

> Derartig enttäuscht, derartig verlangend, derartig verschlossen und verhüllend, derartig zum Aufbrechen und Losbrechen vorbereitet, stöszt Keller bald darauf mit den Weltgedanken überhaupt, mit Philosophie, Religion und Staatsweisheit zusammen. Sein persönliches Lebensschicksal hat ihn zur kalten und trostlosen Ernüchterung geführt, es geleitet ihn aber auch in das Bereich der Ahnungen und der Mystik empor. (p. 27)

Keller's tribulation had given him a certain supremacy over emotionalism, yet had also made him a mystic. His new interest was the salvation of the truly spiritual:

> Es geht ihm ebenso wie dem Genfer Amiel. Sie sind Gegner eines deistischen Symbolismus, weil sie die absolute Gottesidee retten möchten. Christ, Satan, Hölle, alles das ist ein vergröberter Symbolismus, der Geistiges ins Irdische hinunterzieht. Die Kühnheit und Freiheit müssen rückerobert werden, damit das Geistige erfüllt wird. (p. 69)

The years of inner meditation which followed the fatal love for Johanna Kapp had led to the enlightened *Weltanschauung* embodied in the conclusion of the revised *Grüner Heinrich*:

> So läutert sich ein Kopf in den Jahrzehnten, so entwindet er sich langsam aus Fesseln der Phantasie und der Ueberlieferung. (p. 40)

Then suddenly he had become a naturalist:

> Nun empfängt der Greis plötzlich eine Eingebung, die ihn zu ganz andren Bezirken fortreiszt. (p. 18)

Against his will, Keller had become a forerunner of the naturalist school (p. 19): so reasoned Max Hochdorf. However, his inability to bring Keller's "naturalistic" phase into a well-rounded pattern induced him to come forth a few months later with a second work, *Zum geistigen Bilde von Gottfried Keller*, which advanced the new thesis that the two periods in Keller's thought after 1849 were in reality but one. Keller had been a psychological naturalist in attitude ever since the Kapp episode, though he chose to conceal his views for a good part of the time.

---

[18] pp. 20-27, especially p. 27 in Hauch's study.

In this second study, Hochdorf followed a somewhat different procedure. He no longer contrasted the two versions of *Der Grüne Heinrich*. Instead he contrasted the original version with *Martin Salander*. Working back from *Martin Salander* (1886) to *Der Grüne Heinrich* (1855), Hochdorf came to the following conclusion:

> Er (Keller) wollte selbst das Tierische im Menschen entblöszen wie nur ein anderer Naturalist. Man musz einen Augenblick bei dieser Tatsache verweilen. Man musz die ganze Leidenschaft dieser Kunstvision für eine Weile aufspüren, um zu verstehen, dasz Keller davon geträumt hat, *seine neuen Menschengeschöpfe und deren ganze Umwelt nach den sehr handgreiflichen Gesetzen des Naturalismus aufzubauen*. Und nun folgt bei der einsammelnden Beurteilung solcher Aesthetik eine beträchtliche Ueberraschung. *Der planende Greis will für den "Salander" das Gleiche, was der Jüngling für den "Grünen Heinrich" gewollt hat*. Alles was zwischen diesen beiden Büchern liegt ... erscheint wie ein köstliches Abenteuer. Der Dichter hat lustwandelnd Kunststile erprobt, die ihm fremd waren. (p. 85) (my italics)

Hochdorf was still fully aware that works such as the *Sinngedicht* were a defense of the freedom of the spirit. He admitted:

> In solchen Augenblicken wird die Trennung von den Nüchternen und Naturalisten vollzogen. Behauptet wird, dasz ein Mensch "nicht nur vom Glanz der Abendsonne, sondern auch von einem hellen, inneren Lichte" beleuchtet wird. Zu Ehren kommt also wiederum eine Art mystische Hellseherkunst. Von neuem wird die Seele aus ihrer Sklaverei befreit, da sie nicht mehr in heftig umklammernder Gemeinschaft mit dem Körper wohnen musz. (p. 12)

Hochdorf himself raised the question whether such works did not refute his thesis of naturalism:

> Die Frage taucht auf, ob wieder alle Rechte jener Psychologie eingeräumt werden sollen, die jegliches Leben der Seele säuberlich aus den vergänglichen Gebeinen schält und die Kluft zwischen Gebein und Gemüt unüberwindlich macht. (p. 92)

Hochdorf readily conceded the difficulty of the problem involved:

> Eine scharfumgrenzte Antwort auf die Frage wäre eine Unvorsichtigkeit und eine Uebereilung. (p. 93)

For himself, however, Hochdorf was convinced that Keller was basically a naturalist. After balancing the "Gewicht der Kellerschen Stimmungen gegeneinander," he concluded that, even though Keller had mitigated the naturalism of *Der Grüne Heinrich* when he revised it, the full force of *Martin Salander* could not be counteracted (p. 93). Despite all the indications to the contrary, Keller was a naturalist:

> Wohl zweifelt Keller kaum daran, dasz im Menschen ein weithin ausstrahlender Zusammenhang zwischen dem Körperlichen und Geistigen besteht, und dasz die hohen Eigenschaften des Menschen von den niedrigen Vorgängen beherrscht werden. Aber er hat grosze Scheu, das so klipp und klar auszusprechen. (p. 89)

Keller had retained romantic elements in his works to conceal his naturalistic *"Seelenanalyse"* from the masses, who he felt were unsympathetic to such diagnosis:

> Nein, der Menschenfischer, der durch Zerstückelung des Herzens ein Regent über seinesgleichen werden will, trennt sich in allen Erwägungen und Plänen früh von der Romantik. Nehmen sein Geist und Gefühl oder vielmehr die seinen Geist enthüllende Formensprache dennoch in die neue Welt mancherlei Gewohnheiten einer alten Welt hinüber, so sind eben das rein Geistige und der Geschmelz des Gefühls behutsam von den Formgebräuchen des Dichters zu unterscheiden. (p. 97)

Thus Hochdorf concluded his second study. But just as *Martin Salander* had been the sore spot of the first study, the revised *Grüner Heinrich* refused to fit into the naturalistic picture, and it is a tribute to Hochdorf's integrity that he did not seek to force the work into the pattern against his convictions. Hochdorf had to admit that the defense of "Seelenfreiheit" in this work seemed born "aus einer wirklichen Weltanschauung":

> Ihm, dem Künstler, kommt alles darauf an, das Seelenbild der Judith und des Grünen Heinrichs bis in jeden Winkel zu erleuchten ... Denn es ist der Plan des Dichters, dasz jedes der beiden Wesen die Festigung der Welterkenntnis und die Sicherung des Seelenfriedens *in vollkommener Freiheit gewinne.* (p. 76) (my italics)

> Man ist versucht, dem emphatischen Ibsenpriester Brahm recht zu geben, da er zugunsten der Kellerschen Seelenfreiheit die Ibsensche Seelenverengung bemäkelt ... Während Heinrich und Judith den Bezirk ihrer Seelenfreiheit abstecken, öffnet sich die Welt rings um sie sehr weit. Was diese beiden Menschenkinder wollen, ist wie der Wille, den sich alle Menschenkinder, denen ein gleiches Schicksal begegnet, auch aneignen sollten. *Aus einer wirklichen Weltanschauung scheint der Wille von Judith und Heinrich herzustammen* ... (p. 78) (my italics)

Gottfried Kellers Weltanschauung (1921) by A. von Gleichen-Russwurm was another study which used the "romantic-realistic" approach. This fact is clearly seen from Gleichen-Russwurm's discussion of Keller as a young artist:

> In dieser Atmosphäre künstlerischen und auch leise drohenden politischen Kampfes entsteht in Kellers unbefriedigter Seele ein Widerstreit zwischen dem Romantischen und dem typisch Modernen, er schwankt zwischen beiden, und im Abwägen der alten und der neuen Kunstrichtung bildet sich schon damals eine Vereinigung des Realistischen und Phantastichen ihm als künstlerisches Ideal, wie es später in allen seinen Werken den hervorstechendsten Zug ausmachen sollte. (pp. 13-14)

Gleichen-Russwurm attached no importance to Keller's literary production before 1849, stating that Keller's works began with *Der Grüne Heinrich*:

> Am Ein- und Ausgang von Gottfried Kellers Schaffen stehen zwei Romane ... Weltanschauungsromane ... (p. 32)

Gleichen-Russwurm sought a more satisfying formula than Hochdorf had offered, and felt that the common bond between the two works was an attitude of "instinctive realism":

> Mit Dichtern wie Burns, Hebbel, Reuter und Klaus Groth hat er den instinktiven Realismus gemein, der keiner aesthetischen Schulweisheit bedarf, wenn er schildert was er sieht und seine Ueberzeugung am Beispiel erhärtet. (p. 123)

Gleichen-Russwurm took cognizance of both the importance and the complicated nature of Keller's concept of *Freiheit*:

> Er (Keller) trat immer ein für Willensfreiheit und das Recht der Selbstbestimmung gegenüber den willkürlich aufgerichteten Schranken der Macht, aber tief gründete seine Ehrfurcht vor allem wahrhaft ehrwürdigen, vor dem inneren Gesetz, das in der Brust jedes Edlen lebt. (p. 123)

With Ermatinger, however, Gleichen-Russwurm felt that Keller's *Weltanschauung* was essentially political in nature:

> Ein in bescheidenen Grenzen befriedigter Patriotismus, ein gut gefügtes Dasein in die Geschehnisse von Stadt und Land, beherrscht von jenem "wohltemperierten" Liberalismus, der als Erbe des Kulturideals der Aufklärung noch mit dem achtzehnten Jahrhundert zusammenhing, gaben seiner Weltanschauung ein festgefügtes, politisches Gepräge. (p. 121)

Gleichen-Russwurm felt that the only reason Keller's attitude was more staid than that of the German political writers was that he lived "in einem freien Staat . . . in dem die meisten Forderungen jener theoretisch erfüllt waren" (p. 121). In the manner of Ermatinger, Gleichen-Russwurm summed up Keller's life work as purely political: to teach the citizen to accept voluntarily the necessary burdens of social existence:

> So löste sich für ihn aus den Zeitverhältnissen eine psychologische Aufgabe, denn er sah die einzig wahre Reform darin, aus dem Individuum einen Bürger zu entwickeln, geeignet und gewillt, die Notwendigkeiten der gemeinsamen Existenz mit ihren Forderungen auf sich zu nehmen, statt sie, wie es der Hochmütige und der Törichte möchten, widerwillig abzuschütteln. (pp. 123-124)

In 1930 there appeared a study by Edgar Neis, *Romantik und Realismus in Gottfried Kellers Prosawerken*. Neis admitted at the outset that the literary concepts *romanticism* and *realism* were of more importance to him than Keller's *Weltanschauung*. The work was primarily to be a "Beitrag zur Begriffsbestimmung der literarhistorischen Terminologien des XIX Jahrhunderts." In his preface Neis had stressed:

> Diese (Methode) versucht, über den speziellen Fall Gottfried Kellers hinaus, von programmatischer Bedeutung zu sein und steht so als tiefere Absicht überall hinter dem eigentlichen Thema dieser Arbeit.

Neis devoted his main attention to the two versions of *Der Grüne Heinrich*, which were analyzed according to the "fünf Lebensmächte, die den Helden bilden, weil in ihnen die Weltanschauung seiner Zeit und seiner Selbst nach allen Seiten hin sich ausspricht" (p. 33). Neis came to the conclusion that Keller had gone through three stages. First he had been a "schulromantischer Epigone" (till 1853), then a "Künder poetischer Wahrheit" and "Dichter der ewigen Romantik" (1853-1860), and finally he had become a "strenger Realist" (1860——). Keller had developed from "schulromantischem Gebaren zu wirklichkeitsgetreuem Realismus" (p. 96).

Neis accepted Hochdorf's discussion of the *Sinngedicht*[19] and expressed the view that "Freiheit des Geistes" was of key importance to Keller in the second period, revealing his adherence

---

[19] Neis quotes from Hochdorf on page 89.

to the "ewige Romantik." The *Sinngedicht* had eulogized *Freiheit des Geistes*:

> Freiheit des Geistes ist was Lucie proklamiert. Allerdings nicht die Freiheit schulromantischer Geistigkeit, sondern eines Geistes, der über den Dingen schwebt um sie zu besitzen . . . So ist das *Sinngedicht* die Proklamation einer freien Geistesart, wie sie—mit Ausnahme der Landvogt Novelle—kaum in einem andern Werke dieser Epoche so deutlich zum Ausdruck kommt. (p. 88)

This was all Neis had to say on *Freiheit*, however, as he was interested in demonstrating Keller's adherence to the *ewige Romantik* and not in Keller's attitude *per se*.

In 1940 Käthe Heesch in her study, *Der Grüne Heinrich als Bildungsroman des deutschen Realismus*, did little more than redevelop in greater detail the analysis made by Neis. In precisely the same fashion, she examined the two forms of the novel from the point of view of the five categories, substituting, however, *Natur* for *Erziehung*. The categories now were, "*Natur, Religion, Liebe, Kunst und Politik*." Instead of the literary terms *romanticism* and *realism*, she used the terms *Phantasie* and *Wirklichkeit*. Her thesis was the triumph of *Wirklichkeit*. It is interesting to note that Miss Heesch felt young Heinrich's *Naturgefühl* owed little to the romantic tradition, and that she questioned whether there was any romantic element in his early conception of nature:

> Wenn also Heinrichs Naturgefühl offenbar durch das Erbe der Romantik wenig belastet ist, so liegt die Frage nahe, ob in seinem Verhältnis zur Natur überhaupt von einem Spannungszustand zwischen Phantasie und Wirklichkeit die Rede sein kann. (p. 37)

The political approach dealt with Keller, the political idealist. During his life-time, to his own deep regret, Keller had been most esteemed for his political idealism. The trend in recent years, however, has been to place less and less emphasis on the political phase of Keller's attitude, though the subject continues to be rediscussed.

Among the more important works in this category is the three hundred page study which Hans M. Kriesi made in 1918 on *Gottfried Keller als Politiker*. In 1931 a dissertation was published by Ernst Howald on *Gottfried Keller als Schweizer und als Deutscher*. And in 1939, as has already been noted, Jonas Fränkel, the editor of the authoritative Keller edition, discussed *Gottfried Kellers Politische Sendung.*

These are the more recent political studies. All of them note the ubiquitous presence of *Freiheit* in Keller's thought, but only as a political concept. Howald, for example, noted the presence of *Freiheit* even in the nature lyrics. To Howald, however, it was merely political freedom:

> Viele seiner Lieder und Gedichte, in denen er die Schönheiten der Natur preist, verkleiden politische Tagesfragen. (p. 20)

Both Howald and Kriesi discussed Keller's lyrics of freedom in detail, but always as manifestoes of his political thought.

Thus, in all of these studies, Keller was viewed as primarily a political personality concerned with political ideals.

In 1932, Hans Corrodi, in a ten-page discussion of *Gottfried Kellers Weltanschauung,* raised his voice against the limited scope of the critical studies on Keller:

> In allen diesen Formeln steckt ein wahrer Kern, alle aber beleuchten die komplexe Erscheinung nur von einer Seite und ihr innerstes Wesen bleibt im Dunkeln.[20]

Corrodi's conviction was that Keller's literary strength was simply his profound religious experience. This was the creative force in Keller's being:

> Wie tief und innig das religiöse Gefühl in Keller war, das Gefühl der Verbundenheit mit dem Urgrund alles Seins, bewirkt sein *Grüner Heinrich.* Das religiöse Gefühl ist ihm so lebendig, so schöpferisch, dasz es vor allem vor den "eintönigen Gewaltsätzen" der Dogmen zurückscheut.[21]

Corrodi concluded:

> Diese Gottesfurcht, dieses Heimatsgefühl ist es, welche die ganze Kellersche Dichtung wie ein magisches Licht durchflutet . . . er ist ein aus der Urtiefe echten Volkstumes aufgetauchter letzter Mythenschöpfer und Märchenerzähler.[22]

Corrodi's study emphasized the permanent glow in Keller's being, but was no study of *Weltanschauung* as it did little more than to document in chronological order the continued presence of Keller's religious experience.

---

[20] *Zeitwende,* Dec. 1932, p. 443.
[21] *Ibid.*
[22] *Ibid.,* p. 452.

Corrodi's thesis was far from the novelty he believed it to be. Ricarda Huch had already written in 1904:

> Man kann mit dem Verstand und dem Geschmack die verschiedenen religiösen und philosophischen Meinungen billigen, eine, die im Wesen des Menschen begründet ist, bleibt davon unberührt, und das war bei Gottfried Keller die eigentliche Frömmigkeit und Gottgläubigkeit, bestehend in der immer gegenwärtigen Ueberzeugung von der Folgerichtigkeit und Zweckmäszigkeit alles Geschehenden und in der unerschütterlichen Verehrung des Weltganzen.[23]

In 1920 Ermatinger had devoted an entire essay, *Gottfried Kellers Lebensglaube,* to a study of Keller's basic religious experience. Ermatinger had concluded:

> Er war voll Frömmigkeit, wie jeder echte Schöpfer, und die Natur war ihm Gott—ein Gott, tiefer, glühender, reicher, quellender als der ausgebrannte Gottesbegriff, des, wie er meinte, veralteten Christentums und von hier aus wurde er der Dichter seiner Zeit, ein Erwecker des Lebens. In diesem inbrünstigen Lebensglauben spricht sich Gottfried Kellers Verhältnis zu den kosmischen Mächten aus, seine Frömmigkeit. (*Krisen und Probleme*, p. 216.)

In 1921, Gleichen-Russwurm voiced a view which seemed antithetical to that of Ermatinger, as it stressed Keller's "theistisches Fühlen," but which in any case showed an awareness of the powerful religious experience which existed "ungebrochen" in Keller's being:

> Er steht fest und breit auf der Erde, aber sein Gemüt schwelgt in einem ungebrochenen theistischen Fühlen, wie es der grüne Heinrich in sich trägt und wie es Martin Salander nicht von sich weisen kann. Aus diesem Gefühl schöpft Keller jenen seltenen Realismus, der den Trieb zum Idealen einschliesst.[24]

Corrodi may have been reflecting the modern interest in the dynamic subconscious in man, but even here he had a predecessor. In 1907 Hugo von Hofmannsthal had written:

> Die Kraft der Weisheit spielt hier mit dem wüsten Durcheinander des Lebens und bildet daran und läszt ihren Glanz auf allem was sie gebildet hat . . . Dies bewundere ich am höchsten in den Werken dieses Mannes: die Kraft, die allem, selbst dem Albersten,

---

[23] Ricarda Huch, *Gottfried Keller*, p. 25.
[24] *Gottfried Kellers Weltanschauung*, p. 23.

dem Gemischtesten, noch eine Form gibt, vermöge deren es für einen Augenblick lebt und leuchtet.[25]

In his conclusion, Hofmannsthal had summed up as follows:

> Und dasz er dies (irgendeine Bewandtnis mit unglaublich feiner und richtiger Verteilung der Masse und Gewichte) von einer mysteriösen, meinetwegen demiurgischen Kraft ableitet, ist mir auch recht. So erklärt sich's doch einigermaszen, dasz diese Bücher ihre schönste Wirkung, eine seelenhafte Freiheit und Heiterkeit, gar nicht in den Kopf strahlen, sondern wirklich direkt ins Blut . . .[26]

Thus, it may be seen that Corrodi merely reiterated what a number of scholars had already said. He did not furnish the still lacking discussion of the *Weltanschauung* which reflected this persistent inner experience in Keller.

A more specific study of Keller's dynamic essence, based on the philosophic principles of Ludwig Klages, was made by Erwin Ackerknecht in 1937.[27] In this study Keller was analyzed not in terms of the concepts he used but in terms of the feelings he displayed. The categories which Ackerknecht used for this analysis were "Kompositionsbedürfnis," "rhythmisches Grundgefühl," "Ordnungsbedürfnis," "Herbstgefühl," "Bereitschaft zur Mitergriffenheit," "Anfälligkeit des Dichters für seelische Induktionsströme," and so on. Ackerknecht stated that the purpose of his study was to help rescue the German *Seele*. His basic attitude may be designated as lyrical patriotism.

Ackerknecht, by implication, associated Keller's concept of *Freiheit* with "seelische Verbundenheit." He stated that freedom for Keller was clearly not individualism, and backed up this assertion by quoting the passage from *Der Grüne Heinrich* in which Heinrich, after reading Goethe, experienced the inner harmony of all things. Then Ackerknecht had concluded:

> Obwohl in diesen Sätzen nicht ausdrücklich von Individualismus die Rede ist und das Problem zunächst unter den Gesichtswinkel des künstlerischen Ganzheitserlebnisses gerückt ist, wird hier deutlich *die durch seelische Verbundenheit bedingte Bereicherung des Individuums* aus dem Ganzen heraus und ihre Rückwirkung auf das Ganze . . . angedeutet (my italics)

Ackerknecht's stress on *"seelische Verbundenheit"* reflected his implicit thesis that Keller's cultural-political views were

---

[25] *Die prosaischen Schriften gesammelt,* "Ueber die Schriften von Gottfried Keller," p. 23.
[26] *Ibid.,* p. 37.
[27] Cf. p. 146, fn. 14.

identical with the "völkisch" views of pre-war Germany. This implicit thesis is apparent in the following passage:

> Worauf es ihm aber in seinem engeren Vaterland wie im Bereich der groszen Sprachgenossenschaft immer wieder ankam, das war: Volksgemeinschaft soll kein Ruhekissen bedeuten, sondern eine Aufgabe, keine gefühlselige Illusion, sondern das verantwortungsfreudige, unablässige Ringen um ein Ideal, das ein unbestechliches Auge und ein gläubiges Herz erfordert, ein Ringen insbesondere auch um die Erhaltung der stammestümlichen Mannigfaltigkeit, um die Gesunderhaltung des bodenständigen kulturellen Eigenlebens deutscher Gaue. (p. 42)

One might make a detailed study in this passage of the emotional force of the lyrical adjectives such as *verantwortungsfreudig, unablässig, unbestechlich, gläubig*, of the questionable use of political metaphors such as in the contrasting of "engeres Vaterland" with "grosse Sprachgenossenschaft," of the smooth correlation of political ideals which held solely for Switzerland with the larger, purely cultural German unit, and of the unjustified reference to modern Switzerland as a "deutscher Gau." Even without such a study, however, the misleading nature of this passage becomes clear when it is recalled that the *Aufgabe*, referred to throughout, had been for Keller to make all men *Weltbürger*, capable of governing themselves in a democratic world.

It was no doubt Ackerknecht's study among others that incited Jonas Fränkel to write his work *Gottfried Kellers Politische Sendung* (1939), in which he asserted that Keller research in Germany had sacrificed its scientific integrity in order to disseminate propaganda.[28]

Be all of this as it may, it is clear that the modern studies of Keller's dynamic essence have neither made startlingly new contributions nor have they filled the need for a pertinent discussion of Keller's *Weltanschauung*.

Mention should be made of two further studies that do not come under any of the three approaches just discussed. Paul Foucar's *Gottfried Kellers Ethik dargestellt im Grünen Heinrich* (1926) made a material contribution to the literature on Keller's *Weltanschauung* in that it attributed basic importance to Keller's concept of *Freiheit*, conceiving of it as a philosophic

---

[28] It is not implied in this study that Ackerknecht's work was necessarily conscious propaganda.

concept related to his fundamental belief in man's perfectibility. Foucar devoted his first chapter to a discussion of freewill:

> Es wird darin gezeigt, wie Heinrich-Keller den freien Willen zwar nicht psychologisch begründen kann, wie er ihn aber als moralische Kraft, als Herrschaft über das Triebwesen fordert, *denn die damit erlangte persönliche Freiheit des Menschen erkennt er als das höchste Gut.*[29] (my italics)

From this viewpoint, Foucar had wanted to present a picture of Keller's *Weltanschauung*:

> Der leitende Gesichtspunkt war, aus den Handlungen, Erlebnissen und Reden der Romanspersonen vom Standpunkt einer deskriptiven Psychologie aus die Lebensauffassung des Dichters herauszuarbeiten.[30]

Foucar presented, however, solely an account of the ethical principles inherent in *Der Grüne Heinrich*. His highly restricted study with its ethical terminology failed to give Keller's relation to nature and natural law the attention necessary to a well-rounded study of Keller's *Weltanschauung*.

Ricarda Huch's short biographical study of fifty-nine pages, *Gottfried Keller*, might well have presented an adequate treatment of Keller's attitude had it been less brief—the discussion of *Weltanschauung* was condensed in some four pages. Her awareness of Keller's basic religious experiences has already been indicated. She had also noted the basic nature of Keller's interest in *Freiheit*:

> Entgegen den wissenschaftlichen Meinungen, die er hörte, entschied er sich dann auch zugunsten der Willensfreiheit, da er es verschmähte, die Verantwortung für sein Tun und Lassen, auf ein unverantwortliches Unbekanntes abzuwälzen. (p. 28)

Furthermore, she had observed that Keller, though he preserved his intellectual independence, felt the subservience of man to natural law:

> Die Gebundenheit des Menschen erfuhr er auch an sich: aber wenn er sich gehen oder sinken liesz, geschah es in dem Gefühl, dasz er selbst das Zeichen zur Wiedererhebung geben könne. (p. 28)

---

[29] Paul Foucar, *Auszug aus der Dissertation*, (Frankfurt a/M. 1926 (two pages long), p. 2.
[30] *Ibid.*

She had then emphasized the importance of this intellectual independence by quoting as follows from *Der Grüne Heinrich*:

> Mags in der Brust stürmen und wogen, der Atem in der Kehle stocken! Der Kopf soll oben bleiben bis in den Tod! (p. 28)

In one splendid passage, she had noted the relation and significance of Keller's optimism, of his belief in natural law, of his conception of freedom, and of his artistic and completely human love for life:

> Die bekannte Weltbejahung Gottfried Kellers hängt zusammen oder ist eigentlich eins mit seiner Frömmigkeit, die an die Vernunft des Weltganzen glaubt, und weisz, "dasz eher ein Berg einstürzt, als ein Menschenwesen ohne angemessene Schuld zugrunde geht"; mit dem daraus entspringenden Freiheits- und Verantwortlichkeitsgefühl, mittätig in der groszen Lebenswelt zu sein, und schlieszlich mit der Lust an der schönen Erscheinung, ohne die keiner Künstler sein kann. (p. 29)

Thus, as one looks over the critical literature, it becomes clear that of the three types of studies, the romantic-realistic group has supplied the best picture of Keller's *Weltanschauung*, but that even this group has failed to detect the enduring aspects of outlook because of the emphasis placed on the transition in his views.

BIBLIOGRAPHY

I. *Bibliography*

Zippermann, Charles C. *Gottfried Keller Bibliographie 1844-1934*. Zürich: Rascher & Cie, 1935. (This is a comprehensive bibliography of all editions and all critical studies on Keller for the period 1844-1934 inclusive.)

II. *Editions*

(Unless otherwise indicated, reference has been made throughout this study to the Fränkel edition.)

Baechthold, Jakob. *Nachgelassene Schriften und Dichtungen* (Dritte Auflage). Berlin: W. Hertz Verlag, 1893.

Fränkel, Jonas. *Gottfried Kellers Briefe an Vieweg, Schriften der Corona XIX*. Zürich: Verlag der Corona, 1938.

——. *Sämtliche Werke*. Wien, Erlenbach-Zürich: Eugen Rentsch Verlag, 1926-1931. Bern: Benteli Verlag, 1931-1946. (Karl Helbling became editor in 1942. This edition is sponsored by the Canton Zürich and is superior to all earlier editions.)

Hertz, Wilhelm. *Gesammelte Werke*. Berlin: Verlag von W. Hertz, 1889.

III. *Biographies*

Ackerknecht, Erwin. *Gottfried Keller*. Leipzig: Insel Verlag, 1939.

Baechthold, Jakob. *Gottfried Kellers Leben. Seine Briefe und Tagebücher* (Vierte verbesserte Auflage), Bd. I. Berlin: Verlag von W. Hertz, 1895.

Baldensperger, Fernand. *Gottfried Keller, Sa Vie et Ses Oeuvres*. Paris: Lib. Hachette & Cie, 1899.

Ermatinger, Emil. *Gottfried Kellers Leben, Briefe und Tagebücher*, nach Jakob Baechthold (Zweite Auflage). 3 Bde. Stuttgart: Cotta Buchhandlung, 1916.

Frey, Adolf. *Erinnerungen an Gottfried Keller* (Zweite erweiterte Auflage). Leipzig: Verlag von H. Haessel, 1893.

Huch, Ricarda. *Gottfried Keller*. Leipzig: Insel Bücherei, 1904.

Steiner, Gustav. *Gottfried Keller. Sechs Vorträge*. Basel: Helbling und Lichtenhahn, 1918.

IV. Critical Studies

Ackerknecht, Erwin. *Gottfried Keller.* Berlin: Widukind Verlag, 1937. (Uses the "biocentric" approach of Ludwig Klages.)

Beyel, Franz. *Zum Stil des Grünen Heinrich.* Tübingen: J. C. B. Mohr, 1914.

Brahm, Otto. *Gottfried Keller. Ein literarischer Essay.* Berlin: Auerbach, 1883.

Corrodi, Hans. "Gottfried Kellers Weltanschauung," *Zeitwende* (1932), pp. 442-452. München: Beck Verlag.

Dünnebier, Hans. *Gottfried Keller und Ludwig Feuerbach.* Zürich: Ketner Verlag, 1913.

Ermatinger, Emil. "Gottfried Kellers Weltanschauung," *Wissen und Leben* (1911), pp. 271-280, 340-352. Zürich.

———. "Gottfried Keller an der scheide zweier Zeitalter," *Krisen und Probleme der neueren deutschen Dichtung,* pp. 259-286. Zürich: Almathes Verlag, 1928. (Essay written in 1919.)

———. "Gottfried Kellers Lebensglaube" (1919) *Krisen und Probleme* (cf. above), pp. 210-227.

———. "Zwei Dichterworte" (1927), in *Krisen und Probleme* (cf. above), pp. 193-204.

———. *Dichtung und Geistesleben der Deutschen Schweiz,* pp. 624-643. München: Beck Verlag, 1933.

———. "Die Religion Gottfried Kellers" in *Die Tatwelt* (Dec., 1940) pp. 67-81. Berlin: Junker und Dünnhaupt Verlag.

Faesi, Robert. "Gottfried Keller und Goethe. Briefe eines Schweizers an einen deutschen Zeitgenossen," in *Jahrbuch der Goethegesellschaft* (1919), Bd. VI, pp. 59-81. Insel Verlag.

Foucar, Paul. *Gottfried Kellers Ethik dargestellt im "Grünen Heinrich."* Diss. Frankfurt a.M., 1926.

Fränkel, Jonas. *Gottfried Kellers Politische Sendung.* Zürich: Verlag Oprecht, 1939.

von Gleichen-Russwurm, A. *Gottfried Kellers Weltanschauung.* (Philosophische Reihe herausg. von Dr. Alfred Werner, 23 Bd.) München: Rösl & Cie., 1921.

Hauch, Edward F. *Gottfried Keller as a Democratic Idealist.* New York City: Columbia University Press, 1916.

Heesch, Käthe. *Der Grüne Heinrich als Bildungsroman des Deutschen Realismus*. Diss. Hamburg, 1940.

Hochdorf, Max. *Gottfried Keller im europäischen Gedanken*. (Schweizerische Bibliothek No. 14) Zürich: Rascher & Cie., 1919.

——. *Zum geistigen Bilde Gottfried Kellers*. Zürich: Almathea Verlag, 1919.

von Hofmannsthal, Hugo. "Ueber die Schriften von Gottfried Keller," in *Die prosaischen Schriften gesammelt*, II, 21-39. Berlin: S. Fischer Verlag, 1907.

Howald, Ernst. *Gottfried Keller als Schweizer und als Deutscher*. Diss. Minnesota, 1931. Published by Stechert, New York, 1933.

——, *Gottfried Keller, Schweizer, Deutscher, Dichter, Weltbürger*. New York: G. E. Stechert, 1933.

Jaeggi, Frieda. *Gottfried Keller und Jean Paul*. Diss. Bern, 1912. Printed in 1913 by Büchler & Co.

Klinkhammer, Johannes. *Gottfried Kellers Kunstanschauung*. Diss. Giessen, 1928.

Korrodi, Eduard. *Gottfried Keller. Ein Deutscher Lyriker*. Leipzig: Hesse und Becker Verlag, 1911.

Kramer, Priscilla M. *The Cyclical Method of Composition in Gottfried Keller's Sinngedicht*. Ottendorfer Memorial Series of Germanic Monographs No. 26, 1939.

Kriesi, Hans M. *Gottfried Keller als Politiker*. Frauenfeld und Leipzig: Verlag Huber & Co., 1918.

Meintel, Paul R. *Gottfried Keller und die Romantik*. Diss. Bern, 1909. Printed by Leeman & Co., Zürich.

Müller-Gschwend, Gustav. *Gottfried Keller als lyrischer Dichter*. Diss. Strassburg, 1910. Mayer und Müller, Berlin. (Acta Germanica VII, 2.)

Neis, Edgar. *Romantik und Realismus in Gottfried Kellers Prosawerken*. Berlin: Verlag von Emil Ebering, 1930.

Schmiele, Walter. "Gottfried Keller," *Literaturblatt der Frankfurter Zeitung*, Sonntag 19. Juni, 1938. 71 Jahrg. No. 25, S. 8.

Settels, Paul. *Das Symbolische bei Gottfried Keller*. Diss. Koln, 1921. (Maschinenschrift, 264 Seiten) Extract in *Kölner Jahresbuch* (1921), pp. 40-49.

Waldhausen, Agnes. "Gottfried Kellers Grüner Heinrich in seiner Beziehung zu Goethes Dichtung und Wahrheit," *Euphorion* XVI, (1909) pp. 471-497.
Weimann-Bischof, Anna. *Gottfried Keller und die Romantik*. Diss. München, 1917. Printed by Noske Verlag, Borna-Leipzig.
Witkop, Philipp. *Gottfried Keller als Lyriker*. Freiburg i.B.: C. Troemer Universitäts-Buchhandlung, 1911.

V. *Miscellaneous References*

Baer, Lydia. "The Literary Criticism of Ludwig Klages and the Klages School," *Journal of English and Germanic Philology* XI (1941), pp. 91-138.
Feuerbach, Ludwig. *Sämtliche Werke* (Durchgesehen und neuherausgegeben von W. Bolin) Stuttgart: Frommans Verlag, 1903.
von Goethe, J. W. *Sämtliche Werke*, II Abt. Weimar: Hermann Böhlau Verlag, 1893.
Merker und Stammler. *Reallexikon der Deutschen Literatur*. Berlin: Verlag Walter de Gruyter & Co., 1928-1929.
Petersen, Julius. *Die Wissenschaft von der Dichtung*. Bd. I, *Werk und Dichtung*. Berlin: Junker und Dünnhaupt Verlag, 1939.
Richter, Jean Paul. *Werke*. (herausg. von Rudolf Wustman. Kritisch durchgesehene und erläuterte Ausgabe) Leipzig und Wien: Bibliographisches Institut.
Schiller, Friedrich. *Werke (Deutsche National-Litteratur*, Bd. 129) ed. by R. Boxberger. Berlin u. Stuttgart, Verlag von W. Spemann.

www.ingramcontent.com/pod-product-compliance
Lightning Source LLC
Chambersburg PA
CBHW031314150426
43191CB00005B/234